around

LONDON
with
KIDS

by Jacqueline Brown

2nd EDITION
FODOR'S TRAVEL PUBLICATIONS
New York * Toronto * London * Sydney * Auckland

www.fodors.com

CREDITS
Writer: Jacqueline Brown

Series Editors: Karen Cure, Andrea Lehman
Editor: Linda Cabasin
Editorial Production: Tom Holton
Production/Manufacturing: Angela McLean

Design: Fabrizio La Rocca, *creative director*;
Tigist Getachew, *art director*
Cover Art and Design: Jessie Hartland
Flip Art and Illustration: Rico Lins, Keren
Ora Admoni/Rico Lins Studio

ABOUT THE WRITER

While bringing up her two children in London, Jacqueline
Brown has worked on a wide range of consumer magazines.
She is a frequent contributor to *Fodor's London* and other
Fodor's books.

Fodor's Around London with Kids

ISBN 1–4000–1292–9
ISSN 1533–5321
Second Edition

Important Tip

Although all prices, opening times, and other details in this
book are based on information supplied to us at press time,
changes occur all the time in the travel world, and Fodor's
cannot accept responsibility for facts that become outdat-
ed or for inadvertent errors or omissions. So always confirm
information when it matters, especially if you're making a
detour to visit a specific place.

Special Sales

This book is available for special discounts for bulk purchas-
es for sales promotions or premiums. Special editions, including personalized covers, excerpts of existing books, and
corporate imprints, can be created in large quantities for special needs. For more information, write to Special Markets/
Premium Sales, 1745 Broadway, MD 6-2, New York, New York
10019 or e-mail specialmarkets@randomhouse.com. Inquiries
from Canada should be directed to your local Canadian book-
seller or sent to Random House of Canada, Ltd., Marketing
Dept., 2775 Matheson Boulevard East, Mississauga, Ontario
L4W 4P7. Inquiries from the United Kingdom should be sent
to Fodor's Travel Publications, 20 Vauxhall Bridge Road,
London, England SW1V 2SA.

PRINTED IN THE UNITED STATES OF AMERICA
10 9 8 7 6 5 4 3 2 1

COUNTDOWN TO GOOD TIMES

Get Ready, Get Set!
68 Aquatic Experience
67 Art 4 Fun
66 Bank of England Museum
65 Bekonscot Model Village
64 BFI London IMAX Cinema
63 Brass Rubbing Centre
62 British Airways London Eye
61 British Library
60 The British Museum
59 Cabinet War Rooms
58 Camley Street Natural Park
57 Changing of the Guard
56 Chessington World of Adventures
55 Courtauld Gallery
54 Covent Garden
53 *Cutty Sark*
52 Firepower
51 *Golden Hinde*

50 Greenwich Park

49 Hampstead Heath

48 Hampton Court Palace

47 Hawk Conservancy

46 HMS *Belfast*

45 Imperial War Museum

44 Kensington Gardens

43 Kenwood House

42 Kew Bridge Steam Museum

41 Legoland

40 London Aquarium

39 London Butterfly House

38 London Dungeon

37 London's Transport Museum

36 London Wetland Centre

35 London Zoo

34 Madame Tussaud's & London Planetarium

33 Millennium Bridge

32 Monument

31 Mountfitchet Castle

30 Museum in Docklands

29 Museum of London

28 National Army Museum

27 National Gallery

26 National Maritime Museum

25 National Portrait Gallery

24 Natural History Museum

23 Regent's Canal

22 Regent's Park

21 Royal Botanic Gardens

20 Royal Mews at Buckingham Palace

19 Royal National Theatre

18 Royal Observatory

17 St. Paul's Cathedral

16 Science Museum

15 Shakespeare's Globe

14 Somerset House

13 Syon Park

12 Tate Britain

11 Tate Modern

10 Thames Barrier Visitor Centre

9 Theatre Museum

8 Thorpe Park

7 Tower Bridge Experience

6 Tower of London

5 Victoria & Albert Museum

4 Wallace Collection

3 Westminster Abbey

2 Wimbledon Lawn Tennis Museum

1 Windsor Castle

Extra! Extra!

The A-List

Something for Everyone

All Around Town

Many Thanks!

GET READY, GET SET!

Packed with museums, famous buildings, and all kinds of culture, London has appeal for every kid, from tots to teenagers. Since the millennium year, just about every institution in the city has had an interior face-lift, with updated displays and more button-pushing computer games and devices that help kids find out more about what they're seeing. Outside, walks by the Thames or cruises on the river reveal London both old and ultra-new. A ride in an open-top bus gives a sense of the location of the city's neighborhoods and landmarks, or you can simply stroll from park to park to escape the noise and bustle. That's London on the cheap, and if the weather's sunny, at its best.

If you're planning a trip to London, the options can be overwhelming. That's where this book comes in, with 68 ways to have a terrific couple of hours or an entire day, from historic sights to the hands-on, whiz-bang activities of the Science Museum. To ensure that kids don't get culture-dazed, break up a museum day with a picnic in a nearby park or some other outdoor activity. Use the neighborhood directory (All Around Town) and the thematic directory (Something for Everyone) at the back of the book to help you make your plans.

SAVING MONEY

Most national museums and galleries, such as the National Gallery, Science Museum, and National Maritime Museum, have free entry. You'll pay only for special exhibitions. Some attractions offer free admission one day a week or after a certain time in the afternoon (usually an hour or two before closing). Still, London's independent attractions will dig into your wallet big-time. We list only regular adult, student (with ID), and kids' prices, in pounds sterling; children under the ages specified are free. In early 2004, the exchange rate was $1.84 to the pound sterling.

Ask at the ticket booth whether any discounts are offered for a particular status or affiliation (but don't forget to bring your ID). Discounts are often available for senior citizens. Many attractions offer family tickets (usually two adults and two children) or long-term memberships. Prices vary, but the memberships often pay for themselves if you visit several times. Sometimes there are other perks: newsletters or magazines, previews, and shop discounts.

Look for coupons, which might save you £1 per person or provide a child's free admission, and check the attraction's own Web site. Hotel desks often carry Theatre Pair coupons, which allow you to buy two tickets at half price for selected theaters. The TKTS booth, open daily (though Sunday hours are only noon to 3) in Leicester Square, sells selected theater tickets at up to half price for that day's performance. Some groups of attractions (such as Tussaud's and Historic Royal Palaces) offer good-value combination passes. If you're traveling around Britain, look into VisitBritain's Great British Heritage Pass and English Heritage's Overseas Visitor pass.

Consider money-saving tickets for the tube and bus. Different kinds of Travelcards, sold at tube ticket booths, are a good deal. Kids travel free on weekends with the Family Travelcard. Excellent-value Visitor Travelcards, sold only in the United States, can be purchased from BritRail or Rail Europe. Some London passes cover not only attractions but transportation as well. The London Pass includes around 60 attractions, boat and bus trips, and restaurant discounts. It comes in one- to six-day versions and starts at £30 for adults. You can buy the London Pass on the Web (www.londonpass.com), by phone (tel. 0870/242–9988) before you arrive, or from Tourist Information Centres (at Heathrow Airport and Victoria and Liverpool Street stations) and at London Transport Travel Information Centres.

EATING OUT

To save money and still dine well, check out London's many ethnic restaurants. Chinatown is colorful, and the city has many Indian and casual Italian restaurants. Pubs are more budget-wise than fancy restaurants, but not all welcome children in the bar area. Those in this guide have been checked for family-friendliness, and www.pubs.com has more information. Among the more appealing chains for a quick refueling are Pizza Express, Ed's Easy Diner (hamburgers and fries), Pret a Manger (sandwiches and salads), Wagamama (Japanese noodles), and Strada (pizzas). Picnicking in parks is easy; major supermarkets in central locations carry tasty supplies.

GETTING AROUND

London used to be distinct villages, and neighborhoods still retain their individuality. There are 32 different boroughs (administrative districts), and the name of the borough is often given on street signs. Postal (Zip) codes are loosely geographical, radiating from the center (around Marble Arch) and the City financial district. For example, W1 is west of Marble Arch. Bloomsbury, west of the City, is WC1, while the City itself is EC1. Southwark, just south of the Thames, is SE1; Buckingham Palace, north of the river but south of W1, is SW1. Confused? Just pick up a tourist map from a visitor center, buy a *Streetfinder* or *London A–Z* from a newsstand, and get a free tube and bus map from any Underground station, and you'll be fine.

The Underground (tube to Britons, subway to Americans) is the most efficient way of getting around; in-station maps show the train lines. Check which direction you're heading in, and avoid crowded rush-hour trains. Buses are cheaper than the tube but can take longer, although you may enjoy seeing the sights. On some buses, you must prepurchase tickets from machines at the bus stops. Be vigilant with personal belongings and avoid traveling in empty train cars or on the top decks of buses at night. Driving in congested London is a challenge best left to the locals. Pedestrians should watch out for cars—remember, Britain drives on the left, so cars will be coming from the opposite direction.

WHEN TO GO
With the exception of seasonal attractions, kid-oriented destinations are generally busiest when children are out of school—especially weekends, holidays, and summers. Attractions that draw school trips can be swamped with clusters of kids, but school groups leave by early afternoon, so weekdays after 2 during the school year can be an excellent time to visit museums, zoos, and aquariums. London's attractions can be particularly crowded during half-term school vacations (generally the third week of October, last week of December, first week of January, third week of February, last week of March, and first week of June). Outdoor attractions may be less crowded after a rain.

The hours listed are the basic hours, not necessarily those applicable on public, or "bank" holidays. Some attractions close when schools close, but others add extra hours. Surf the Web; some places may have cool special events if they're open on holidays.

LEARNING ENGLISH
You'll get into the British swing of things in no time. Popular kids' food choices include bangers and mash (sausage and mashed potatoes), fish-and-chips (fried fish

and french fries), and, to be extra confusing, crisps (potato chips). "Brilliant" is an oft-heard word for "wonderful," and "trainers" are "sneakers." Referring to transportation, "single" means "one-way," and "return" means "round-trip." Make a detective game of it with your kids, and have fun figuring out the meanings of all the phrases you hear. Brilliant.

RESOURCES AND INFORMATION
The London Tourist Information Centre at Victoria Station Forecourt, and the Britain and London Visitor Centre (1 Regent St.), near Piccadilly Circus, are good resources, with leaflets from independent operators. Check out VisitLondon's Web site, www.visitlondon.com, for information and deals, and VisitBritain's site, www.travelbritain.org. Kids can look at www.kidslovelondon.com, a VisitLondon site written by kids for kids. London Line (tel. 09068/663344), updated daily, is full of prerecorded visitor information; it costs 60p per minute, however. London's weekly *Time Out* magazine has special sections for kids and families.

FINAL THOUGHTS
Lots of moms and dads were interviewed to create these suggestions, and we'd love to add yours. E-mail us your kid-friendly additions at editors@fodors.com (specify the name of the book on the subject line), or write to us at Fodor's Around London with Kids, 1745 Broadway, 15th floor, New York, NY 10019. In the meantime, have fun!

— Jacqueline Brown

AQUATIC EXPERIENCE

In the wild west of London's huge Syon Park (*see #13*), Aquatic Experience is home to a weird, wonderful collection of about 200 exotic and intriguing beasts: saltwater and freshwater creatures plus a handful of landlubbers. The unifying theme here is that the animals were rescued or represent endangered species, from tiny monkeys to lumbering crocodiles. If possible—but obviously not with the crocodiles—you can meet and pet them.

Dedicated keepers, who you may suspect would probably eat and sleep with their charges if they could, answer questions and encourage you to encounter these well-cared-for animals, each of which has its own personality. Mango the cheerful cockatoo—his gorgeous plumage explains his name—likes to walk on your arm, which is fine if you don't mind the occasional pricks from his long claws. If you are very privileged, he might let you caress him under his wing. The monitor lizard, another character, is often taken for a walk in the yard, although he's a little less receptive to petting. The tortoises, however, which lumber about in an open pen, just love attention. At children's parties (animal-encounter parties

KEEP IN MIND The nearby London Butterfly House (*see #39*) has more than 1,000 butterflies as well as other creepy crawlies. Separate admission is charged. You also have to pay extra to enter Syon's gardens, across the parking lot (*see* Syon Park), but the fabulous space, lakes, and floral and arboreal beauty are well worth it. If you want to cram in everything, allow a good hour for the Aquatic Experience, another hour for the butterflies, and at least twice that for the park. If you don't have that much time, perhaps some of your group want to see the butterflies while the rest visit here.

Syon Park, London Rd.,
Brentford. Rail: Syon La.

 £3.50 ages 16 and up,
£2.75 children 4–15

Daily 10–5:30

020/8847–4730;
www.aquatic-experience.org

 3 and up

are favorites here) and other times (check at the admission desk), Ozzie the owl performs flying feats. In one trick, he passes over a line of children lying side by side on the ground—although this sometimes proves a little too close for comfort for tiny tots.

The deadlier creatures are kept behind glass, from the tiny, finger-size Amazon frog, which looks cute but emits a deadly poison, to coiled-up pythons and crocs. On the aquatic front, there's a deep tank with koi and catfish, and you can feed the fish with the keeper (the admission desk has times). In a shallow rock pool, tiny terrapins climb out to greet you, and if you are very gentle, you can stroke their shells.

For some action after all this gazing and encountering, visit the small play area within Aquatic Experience or head to the wide-open spaces of Syon Park.

EATS FOR KIDS
It's too far to walk to leave Syon Park for lunch, but luckily there are good options within the park (*see* London Butterfly House).

HEY, KIDS! What's the difference between a crocodile and an alligator? They both belong to the same family group, crocodilians, which has been around for 200 million years. The way to tell them apart is by their teeth, although since they have eaten humans, you won't want to get close enough to inspect them. But just so you know, alligators don't have those two fiendish lower incisors visible when their jaw is closed. There are also two other related species: caimans, belonging to the alligator group, and the lesser-known gavial, which has a long, slender, snout-shape mouth, with plenty of sharp upper teeth visible, even when shut.

ART 4 FUN

Let your imagination go bananas—or dotty, stripey, fishy, or any other way inspiration takes you! At this creative café–cum–art workshop, you can paint onto a mug, plate, eggcup, vase, or any of about 100 other ceramic pieces and make your own souvenir or gift. Other artistic options involve working with textiles, wood, glassware, and paper. Expertise is not required, only enthusiasm.

The whole spectrum of colors is available for your ceramic venture, and friendly assistants are on hand to help you with the basics, such as how to plan your work, how to draw outlines effectively, and how to apply dark colors last. You can use brushes, sponges, stencils, or fingertips. For inspiration, browse the examples on walls and shelves, and pay attention to the helpful do's and don'ts. The ceramics (which include some Gucci designs) are plain biscuit ware, which is then glazed and fired after you're finished designing. The main drawback is that this takes a couple of days, so if you won't be around; the finished work will have to be mailed to your home. All ceramic tableware is microwave- and dishwasher-safe.

HEY, KIDS!
The helpful staff at Art 4 Fun won't throw you out if you are too busy having fun. Late-night parties have been known to get pretty colorful. Some children even come in pjs, making a pajama party with a difference.

KEEP IN MIND The cost of your project is based on the particular piece you choose in addition to a flat studio space fee per person for as long as you wish to stay. This is the most central branch of Art 4 Fun. Others are at 44 Chiswick High Road, W4; 172 West End Lane, West Hampstead, NW6; and 212 Fortis Green Road, Muswell Hill, N10. Details on all of these can be obtained by checking the Web site or calling tel. 020/8994–4800.

196 Kensington Park Rd., W11.
Tube: Notting Hill Gate

020/8959-7373;
www.Art4Fun.com

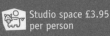 Studio space £3.95
per person

 Daily 10–6, later if reserved

4 and up

If you want to take a completed piece away with you, how about a super silk tie or a pillowcase? Several designs are available, from bold abstract shapes to a more conservative small repeating pattern. All you have to do is choose the colors and paint them on. You can also make a mosaic picture frame or mirror frame, which involves making color selections and lots of sticking.

The mood at Art 4 Fun is very relaxing. Music plays in the background, and there's the gentle buzz of other people working. You can also buy drinks and snacks to help the creative juices flow. Mom and dad can drink coffee while the kids do all the work, or, more likely, parents can catch the creative bug themselves and grab a paintbrush. You can make an inexpensive family evening out by bringing takeout (if you bring wine, there's a small charge for the corkage) to feast on while you design your own dishes.

EATS FOR KIDS While you're in Notting Hill, a bohemian area of London, check out the Portuguese quarter. The **Lisboa Patisserie** (57 Golborne Rd., tel. 020/8968–5242) and **Oporto** (62A Golborne Rd., tel. 020/8968–8839) are typical Portuguese cafés—*pastelarias*—selling budget meals and snacks, from sandwiches and cheese and fish dishes to sweet, custardy pastries. For traditional sausage, cabbage, and bean hot dishes, try **Café Algarve** (129A Ladbroke Grove, tel. 020/7727–4604). If these don't appeal, there are many more places between here and Kensington.

BANK OF ENGLAND MUSEUM

Together, the proud, white pillared facades of the Royal Exchange, the Lord Mayor's Mansion House residence, and the Bank of England, encircling the junction of Threadneedle, Cornhill, Poultry, and King William streets, present an image of power and heritage that leaves you in no doubt that this is Britain's commercial heart. The museum, just around the corner from the bank's entrance, is all you might imagine it would be, from the heavy metal door and lofty domed ceiling to the dapper gatekeeper in top hat and tails. Sadly, he is not your guide. Instead, follow the arrows on the leaflet and children's information sheets, and the story of the bank unfolds.

The original interior of the Bank Stock Office, designed by Sir John Soane in 1793 (Soane's own beautifully preserved house is in Lincoln's Inn), has been re-created, with heavy wooden cupboard desks, glowing embers in the fireplace, and waxwork clerks and bank patrons. Correspondence from celebrated customers is displayed, and the letters from George and Martha Washington make interesting reading.

EATS FOR KIDS The **Place Below** (Cheapside, tel. 020/7329–0789), in the vaults beneath St. Mary-le-Bow church, is a popular vegetarian café that serves quiches, pasta dishes, and desserts. Near the foundations of the Roman Temple of Mithras, **Starbucks** (1 Poultry, Unit 10A, tel. 020/7489–1994) sells good coffee and hot chocolate, well-filled sandwiches, cakes, and muffins. A few steps farther on, **Silks & Spice** (Temple Court, 11 Queen Victoria St., tel. 020/7248–7878) prepares pan-Asian food and has a practical, budget Oriental Express lunch: one-plate dishes (seafood, meat, or vegetables) with rice for £5–£6.

Bartholomew La., off Threadneedle St., EC2.
Tube: Bank

 020/7601–5545 recording;
www.bankofengland.co.uk

 Free

M–F 10–5; Lord Mayor's Show
2nd Sa in Nov

9 and up

The stories of money and the bank are shown through a series of displays. There are cases of notes (bills) and coins of all shapes and sizes from as early as the late 17th century, when the bank was chartered by King William and Queen Mary. Exhibits tell the tale of the hapless souls who tried to counterfeit bank notes: their sentence was death by hanging. Touch screens provide the more technical information about money production, and videos show how design innovations can frustrate forgers. And, of course, there are bars of gold.

As the bank grew in power, it was caricatured in newspapers as a strict matriarch, "the old lady of Threadneedle Street," tightening the purse strings against the whims of monarchs and governments. Today, London remains an important financial center. The final interactive system lets you take the hot seat at a trading desk at an international currency exchange market. You pit your wits against market disasters to succeed in a financial balancing act.

KEEP IN MIND

Special activities for kids are organized during vacations. You might catch Grunal the story-telling money coiner in period costume, minting coins the ancient way with die and hammer. Come on Lord Mayor's Show day and have a coin made for you.

HEY, KIDS! Did you know gold was used to make people feel good—literally? Alchemists mixed powdered gold into drinks to treat arthritis, and it is still used to ease the complaint today. If you want to grab the gold bars, try the tempting stack that lets you compare ancient and modern types by price and weight. Today's version weighs more than 399 ounces and is valued at around £84,000 ($142,550). But stay cool—all the bars are copies except two real bars, one of which you can touch, the only place in Britain where you can do so.

BEKONSCOT MODEL VILLAGE

This magical place all started with Roland Callingham's passion for making models in his garden. He built a model village that was (and is) a little slice of 1930s England, whereupon friends begged him to open it to the public. Seventy years later and now occupying almost 2 acres, the world's oldest model village remains popular with children *and* grown-ups.

Even though there aren't many buttons to push—Bekonscot relies on old-fashioned charm—kids love discovering all that's hidden here, so take your time. (Meanwhile, you can marvel at the craftsmanship.) A work sheet helps kids hunt down objects and points out details. If you follow the little marked pathway, you won't miss a thing.

Just about anything that can be is in miniature here, from a grimy colliery, where a conveyor belt brings chips of coal up from a mine, to a zoo, a castle, a church, pubs, and stately Hanton Court Maze, which has tiny hedges being clipped by a gardener. Notice that some names are tongue-in-cheek, such as Jerry Builder and Dan D. Lyon (the florist).

KEEP IN MIND This isn't an activity for a wet day, as the model village and playground are outside. The village is about an hour from Marylebone station by train. Bekonscot is still managed by the Church Army, an organization like the Salvation Army, which gives proceeds to needy causes.

HEY, KIDS! For a birthday treat, the young Princess Elizabeth (now the Queen) visited Bekonscot. Bert Gray, a model maker here for more than 60 years, was working at Bekonscot on that day. In 1997, he was honored by the Queen for duties to his country, and she recalled visiting the village for her ninth birthday. Bert replied, "I think you'll find it was your eighth birthday, ma'am." Her Majesty graciously admitted that he could be right!

Warwick Rd., Beaconsfield.
Rail: Beaconsfield

 01494/672919;
www.bekonscot.com

 £4.80 ages 16 and up,
£3 children 3–15

 Mid-Feb–Oct, daily 10–5

3 and up

Kids tend to like the moving models best. You can watch for ages as little trains trundle through tunnels and stop at stations. Over a year they travel 16,000 miles around this tiny circuit. In the Maryloo signal box, a full-size human works the controls. At the harbor below, fish are for sale, with dinky vegetables in the shop next door. If you can get on your knees and press your face against the Tudor leaded-glass window of Splashynge Hall, you'll glimpse its tasteful furnishings. At the fairground, not a great deal has changed, as the Ferris wheel, chair swings, and other spinning, whizzing rides are still popular today.

A later addition to Bekonscot is a memorial miniature to children's author Enid Blyton, who lived at Beaconsfield for more than 30 years and whose works are as popular in Britain as Beatrix Potter's or Roald Dahl's. She is busy at her typewriter in the garden. And there goes Noddy, one of her characters, in his famous little yellow car—aaahhh.

EATS FOR KIDS Hot and cold snacks are available from the **kiosk**. In Beaconsfield old town, about 20 minutes' walk, the **Old White Swan** pub (London End, tel. 01494/673800) serves daily specials in wooden booths; kids are welcome until 7 PM. Try the chili and rice, spinach and mushroom lasagna, or Swan burgers (pure beef—no swan!). Children's meals include golden tiddlers (tiny fried fish shapes), chicken nuggets, sausages, and burgers. In the new town, **Jungs** (6 The Broadway, 01494/673070) is much closer and serves chicken, pasta dishes, and salads, with kids' menus.

BFI LONDON IMAX CINEMA

Space-age conservatory or a UFO grounded on the South Bank? From the minute you see this huge cylindrical glass building with a color-splashed mural and foliage-covered tentacles, you know you're in for something special. On the South Bank of the River Thames, this dynamic part of the British Film Institute is set among a number of innovative buildings. A trip to the movies here—whether you're seeing a 3-D show or a more traditional two-dimensional one—provides an experience that's weird, fascinating, and thrilling.

The first tip-off to the size of the screen, the largest in Britain, is that you take an elevator to reach your seat. Sitting at about mid-screen level, you can't help but feel like a dot on the landscape. When the show starts, you are sucked up into the sound, which appears to blast from every angle. This is because the screen's surface has millions of holes that allow the sound from 44 loudspeakers to surround the audience. Together with the high-tech visual effects, the show becomes a virtual reality that pulls you into the on-screen world. Perhaps you'll "dive" down to the *Titanic* (where you may shrink back into your seat to

EATS FOR KIDS The spacious glass-and-steel, ground-floor **café** is a great place to watch the world go round, through floor-to-ceiling windows that double as the curved walls of this cylindrical building. Snack on ices, chocolate fudge cake, carrot cake, and pre-packed sandwiches, daily 11–8:45. Gabriel's Wharf and its eateries (*see* HMS *Belfast*) are a brisk riverside walk away. Here you'll find **Studio Six** (tel. 020/7928–6243), a clap-board hut with a great buzz and fun food, including yummy fries. The moderately priced menu changes daily and includes pasta and fish cakes. Staff are happy to split portions between kids.

1 Charlie Chaplin Walk, SE1.
Tube: Waterloo

020/7902-1234;
www.bfi.org.uk/imax

£7.50 ages 17 and up,
£4.95 children 5-16

Daily, call for show times

3 and up

avoid fish seeming to swim into your face), join an expedition up Mount Everest, or blast into space and walk weightlessly beside astronauts on the moon.

Watching in 3-D can make some people feel a bit motion sick, as the camera swoops frequently to emphasize movement. For these films, you are given dark plastic glasses to wear, which adjust the screen picture; without them you see layers of blurred images. IMAX works with two projection systems, each rolling different film reels: one shows the left-eye image and the other, the right-eye one. The glasses polarize the alignment, in the same way as the projection lenses do. So why can't all movies look so great? The process is very expensive, requiring special film and cameras along with the screening equipment, which makes seeing a 3-D film a rare treat.

KEEP IN MIND
Some films have been made with the help of other London institutions (at which you can encounter some marvels shown in the films), such as the London Aquarium (see #40), for *Into the Deep*, and the British Museum (see #60), for *Mysteries of Egypt*.

HEY, KIDS! Everything about the IMAX is larger than life. It would take 90 London taxis parked next to one another to cover the movie screen and five double-decker buses stacked on top of each other to equal the height of the screen. The IMAX projector, larger and more powerful than a conventional one, weighs 4,200 pounds. Even the film reels are enormous, weighing in at 191 pounds each. Ready for another big-screen experience? The Science Museum (see #16) also has an IMAX screen.

BRASS RUBBING CENTRE

With its concerts, café, and bookshop, St. Martin-in-the-Fields is one of London's most charismatic churches, appealing even to kids. Bordering Trafalgar Square, it was known as the royal parish church, as many baby monarchs were christened within. Down in the bustling crypt is the Brass Rubbing Centre, where you can rub a brass to create a color image of a knight in armor, a gracious lady, a grizzly mythological beast, or an intricate Celtic pattern. The country's monumental brasses—memorial plaques—from the Middle Ages are world famous and graced all the ancient churches in the land.

The brasses on display are replicas of some of England's and Europe's best engraved memorial plaques. (Copies are used in order to preserve the originals, which were walked on and rubbed by enthusiasts for centuries.) These plaques were made for the well-to-do as early as the 11th century (notice the distinctly Norman names, such as the noble-sounding Sir John D'Abernoun, from Surrey) and provided an eternal saintly image to which the living could pray. They produced less clutter in churches than tombs and huge stone

KEEP IN MIND Free lunchtime concerts of classical music are given at the church every Monday, Tuesday, and Friday, as is a regular (admission charged) evening program. Concerts by candlelight are beautifully atmospheric. Details are available in the crypt. After concerts and on Saturdays, the crypt gets really busy.

EATS FOR KIDS To those Londoners in the know, the **Café in the Crypt** (tel. 020/7839–4342) is celebrated for its no-nonsense, budget-price menu, which changes daily. There are usually two hot meat or fish dishes (£5–£7) and a vegetarian option with homely English puds, a.k.a. puddings or desserts (around £2). All profits go back to the church, which sponsors a charity for the homeless. See also the National Gallery and National Portrait Gallery.

St. Martin-in-the-Fields, Trafalgar Sq., WC2.
Tube: Charing Cross, Leicester Sq.

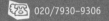 020/7930-9306

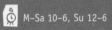 Free; image making
£5 ages 13 and up, £4
children 12 and under

M-Sa 10-6, Su 12-6

7 and up

statues, and were cheaper, too. Note the changes in fashion, both in clothes and in armor. For instance, chain mail graduates to plate armor—for better protection against increasingly effective weapons.

You can choose from more than a hundred images, including such famous kings and queens as Henry VIII, Charles I, and Elizabeth I. The staff prepares your black or white paper, shows you how to make an outline and the first gentle rub with special metallic wax crayons, and how to correct your blips. It's easy once you get the hang of it. Allow at least 30–40 minutes to make a neat job. While kids are busy, adults can explore the church upstairs (designed by James Gibbs, a protégé of Sir Christopher Wren) or rub as well. The shop sells artists' images of the brasses if your efforts don't seem up to par.

HEY, KIDS! After you've completed your brass rubbing, see if you can read some of the worn tombstones on the floor of the crypt. Although people are no longer buried here, there are some famous tombs, such as those of Nell Gwynn (Charles II's mistress) and Jack Sheppard, a notorious highwayman. Search for one tomb by the concert information desk; it has a wonderful skull and crossbones.

BRITISH AIRWAYS LONDON EYE

For an unrivaled bird's-eye view of London, climb aboard the world's largest observation wheel. One of the most dramatic and exciting additions to the London skyline on the vibrant South Bank, the 443-foot-tall, Ferris-like wheel takes you on a 30-minute "flight," with views over the city that, on a clear day, can extend to 25 miles away.

The flight appeals to both young and old, and though from a distance (you can see the wheel from most London bridges and high points) the Eye looks a little scary, don't worry. The 25-person observation capsules are so spacious and comfortable and travel so slowly that you shouldn't feel motion sickness or claustrophobia. In fact, the Eye doesn't really stop, even as you embark, except for visitors in wheelchairs. Inside, you can stand, walk around, or sit on the central bench and view London from a completely new perspective.

To the west, Big Ben is a stone's throw across the river, along with the Houses of Parliament and what most kids call James Bond's headquarters: MI6, the government's secret service.

KEEP IN MIND Lines can be long at peak summer vacation time, but you shouldn't have to wait for longer than 30 minutes. Tickets are sold on a timed basis, but even with a ticket you'd be wise to show up 30 minutes before departure. You can call for advance tickets at least three days early (and then pick up your tickets the day of your trip), book online, or purchase same-day or advance tickets in person from County Hall, adjacent to the Eye. Operating times vary each year, so check ahead.

County Hall, SE1.
Tube: Waterloo, Westminster

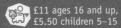 £11 ages 16 and up,
£5.50 children 5–15

 End Jan–Apr and Oct, daily 9:30–8;
May–Sept, M–Th 9:30–8, F–Su 9:30–9
(later June–Aug)

0870/500–0600;
www.ba-londoneye.com

 3 and up

Beyond are Nelson's Column and Buckingham Palace. To the east, you can see Somerset House, OXO Tower, Tate Modern, St. Paul's Cathedral, the Old Bailey law courts, the HMS *Belfast,* Canary Wharf, and the now-closed Millennium Dome. The archbishop's Lambeth Palace is just south of the Eye; the green spaces of Hampstead Heath and the spire of Highgate's village church lie to the north. Other highlights include the radio mast of Crystal Palace and Windsor Castle. You can survey the curvy Thames and its many bridges, the many different colors of rooftops, and the city's usually private inner squares and courtyards.

Upon emerging from the wheel, you may want to go around again sometime. Next time try a magical nighttime flight or one at dusk. If you walk by the Eye then, you'll see myriad camera flashes as people try to capture the moment from the topmost capsules.

EATS FOR KIDS
The **Costa,** a café booth by the lineup area, sells light snacks and great coffee. Walk along the river to Gabriel's Wharf and its restaurants (*see* BFI London IMAX Cinema *and* HMS Belfast).

HEY, KIDS! Although the London Eye looks like a Ferris wheel (named after the 19th-century U.S. engineer G. W. G. Ferris), it's much more than that. Ferris wheels are supported on both sides of the wheel, but this wheel, spectacularly overhanging the river, is supported by an A frame on just one side. Capsules are fixed to the outside of the wheel and are individually motorized so that no part of the structure restricts your view.

BRITISH LIBRARY

This is not a library where you can check out the latest Harry Potter book (it's not a lending library at all, but rather used for reference and research); still, you can discover some pretty magical things here. Take the building itself. It has a broad Mediterranean-type piazza entrance with an Anne Frank memorial tree, and inside, the light, white interior has staircases and escalators that lead to countless reading rooms. The library has a calming atmosphere, one that makes any child with an interest in reading want to investigate further.

In addition to books, journals, manuscripts, stamps, patents, sound recordings, printed music, and maps from recent centuries, this national library holds works from almost 3,000 years ago. The John Ritblat, or Treasures, Gallery brings some of these precious items to the public eye. You can listen to some weird and wonderful extracts from the National Sound Archives, including the voice of Florence Nightingale, an extract from the Beatles' last tour interview, and rare birdsong. On display are many letters on thick, worn paper

KEEP IN MIND The Workshop of Words, Sound and Images is an interactive gallery tracing the story of book production. Free demonstrations of book binding and calligraphy take place most Saturdays, and you can try your skill. Call ahead or check the Web site for details.

EATS FOR KIDS The library's first-floor **restaurant** has a hot dish of the day and a daily soup, plus sandwiches and pastries. As you munch, you can gaze at the leather, gold-lettered spines of books from George III's library. If it's nice outside, relax in the relative peace of the piazza with a snack from the **Chapter Coffee Shop** by the main entrance, while the traffic roars by on Euston Road. Heading back into the West End? Walk down Mabledon Place opposite the library for about five minutes to the **Valencia** (74 Marchmont St., tel. 020/7713–0269) for sandwiches and cappuccino.

96 Euston Rd., NW1.
Tube: Euston, King's Cross

 020/7412-7332; www.bl.uk

 Free; charge for special exhibitions

M and W-F 9:30-6, T 9:30-8, Sa 9:30-5, Su 11-5

 10 and up

in browned ink, including one written by Gandhi during his fast in 1943; Admiral Nelson's last letter to his lover Emma, along with a lock of his hair; and one in secret cipher written by Charles I during the British Civil War. Other holdings on view are a copy of the First Folio of William Shakespeare's plays and manuscripts by Leo Tolstoy, Honoré de Balzac, and Jane Austen. Among the composers' scores, several inches thick, are creations by Handel and Bach—quite a contrast to the Beatles' felt-tip scribblings on scraps of paper. Some sacred texts have survived as fragments, on pieces of papyrus, cotton, and palm leaf. Though it's not possible to run your fingers over these thick old manuscripts, you can use Turning the Pages, a computer screen simulation that lets you leaf through books, such as Leonardo da Vinci's notebooks, page by page. Towering in the center of the building is a six-story glassed-in column that houses the library of King George III. It contains 65,000 books, mainly reference tomes—a fitting heart to this huge library with more than enough for even hardened bookworms.

HEY, KIDS! One of the library's most amazing possessions is the Sherborne Missal, a book that dates to 1400; a missal has everything said or sung at masses throughout the year. It contains almost 700 pages, each produced entirely by hand, with drawings of birds and figures from daily life in England six centuries ago. The attention to detail is beautiful, and the missal is a weighty volume in more ways than one; at 44 lbs it is as heavy as a small child. See the missal in the Treasures Gallery and "turn" some of its pages on a computer screen.

THE BRITISH MUSEUM

Walking through the towering colonnaded entrance and into the spectacular glass-domed Great Court, you may well feel as if you're visiting some great temple. That's not far from reality, as the museum is a shrine to objects from civilizations around the globe. It's so vast that in one visit you can sample only a tiny bite of the pie. Before you come, it's helpful to surf the Children's Compass and Ancient Civilizations on the Web site. Head for the Reading Room, wrapped between sweeping stone staircases at the heart of the Great Court. Beneath its azure dome, scholars like Karl Marx have toiled; it is now techno-equipped and should be your first stop to see what's available for families, such as free pamphlets with trails that guide you to famous or obscure exhibits.

The mummies are always a popular choice, and in the Roxie Walker Galleries attractive displays demystify the unusual rituals of the ancient Egyptians, including gruesome yet practical methods for preserving bodies. Imaging techniques let you actually see inside one mummy's wrappings to see the bones. You can also see mummified animals.

EATS FOR KIDS At the **Court Café** you can people-watch while munching on sandwiches and sticky patisserie. With repro Greek-battle wall friezes, the **Gallery Café** serves hot meals and salads, including kids' options (often sausages and chicken nuggets), after noon, and sandwiches and snacks from 10 AM. Opposite the main entrance, **Pizza Express** (30 Coptic St., tel. 020/7636-3232) has a streamlined Italian bistro setting; obliging staff and good-value pizza, pasta, and salads fill the bill. Minimalist, canteen-style **Wagamama** (4A Streatham St., tel. 020/7323-9223), part of a popular chain, serves filling noodle and rice dishes from £5 up.

Great Russell St., WC1. Tube: Holborn, Russell Sq., Tottenham Ct. Rd.

 £2 suggested donation

 Museum Sa–W 10–5:30, Th–F 10–8:30; Great Court Th–Sa 9 AM–11 PM, Su–W 9–6

020/7323–8000; www.thebritishmuseum.ac.uk

6 and up

Brought to England in 1816 by Lord Elgin, the marble sculptures of Greek gods and warriors that lined the Parthenon in Athens 2,500 years ago are among the greatest gems of the museum. (They're controversial as well, since Greece would like them back.) In a side room, imaging wizardry shows how the riders in the fabled frieze might have looked; there's a special touchable section for kids.

You can discover the people who lived in Britain thousands of years ago, including an actual 1st-century AD example: Lindow Man, who was perfectly preserved in a peat bog. Close by is the Sutton Hoo haul of brooches, swords, and helmets that may have belonged to Redwald, king of the Angles in the 7th century. Another section of the museum has exhibits on early North Americans, including the headdress of Yellow Calf. Near these displays you can also see Aztec mosaics, and just downstairs are treasures from Africa.

KEEP IN MIND
Because of the museum's huge size, allow at least two hours for a first visit. Sundays can be quite crowded and are best avoided. The children's shop in the Great Court is a good place to buy unique souvenirs.

HEY, KIDS! The awesome glass-and-steel-ceiling Great Court, which links the museum to the azure-and-gold domed Reading Room, was completed in 2000. Check out the amazing roof of the court, which consists of 3,500 triangles of glass— enough for about 500 garden greenhouses. If that doesn't seem like a lot to you, imagine what the Reading Room was once like. After it was built in the 1850s, the whole 2-acre public courtyard was taken over by miles of shelves of books, now housed in the British Library (see #61).

CABINET WAR ROOMS

During World War II, this warren of rooms below the government offices of Whitehall was the nerve center of military operations. Prime Minister Winston Churchill, along with the most important people in the military and government, worked and slept in this secret bunker while the German Luftwaffe attacked the streets above. Today you can tour these historic rooms, some preserved exactly as they were when the war ended. It's as if time stood still—literally. The clocks all read two minutes to five, and background sounds include wailing sirens, voices, footsteps in the corridors, and the tap-tap of busy typewriters. It makes for an eerie atmosphere but an informative visit.

A free audio guide explains about daily life from room to room. (Some of the anecdotes are really funny.) You can see top secret places, including the tiny room—a converted broom closet—in which Churchill made frequent telephone calls to President Roosevelt. Because staff worked and slept in shifts around the clock, the manual typewriters had specially muffled keys to keep their incessant tapping from waking sleepers, especially Churchill.

HEY, KIDS! Keep your eyes open in the kitchen and you might see a mousetrap. Mice (and rats, too) were regular visitors below ground, and to help control these unwelcome guests, Churchill took in a stray cat, naming it after another great leader: Nelson.

EATS FOR KIDS The walls of the **Switchroom** cafeteria are lined with photos of a devastated London, a reminder of what happened above ground during wartime bombing. Sandwiches, soup, and drinks are sold. For a full hot meal, head to the junction of Horse Guards Road and Birdcage Walk, to the ornate Central Hall, opposite Westminster Abbey. In the crypt of the hall, the **Wesley Café** (Storey's Gate, tel. 020/7222–8010) has a limited daily menu from £4.75. Also see Westminster Abbey.

Clive Steps, King Charles St., SW1.
Tube: Westminster, Exit 6

 £7 ages 17 and up

 Apr–Sept, daily 9:30–6; Oct–Mar,
daily 10–6; last admission 5:15

 020/7930–6961;
www.iwm.org.uk

 8 and up

It was a tough job being Churchill's secretary, as his slight speech impediment and impatience could make him more than a little difficult. You can read for yourself some of his many speeches, complete with his own handwritten corrections. The BBC microphones are the ones used when he made his morale-boosting broadcasts to troops and folks at home.

The Map Room is probably the most compelling, because you get a real sense of the theater of war. Every pin, page, and book remains as it was in the height of activity, when heads of state and the military plotted troop movements across the world. You can view the campaigns of the U.S. seaborne forces by map, from the Atlantic to the Far East. During school vacations, costumed actors perform interactive briefing sessions. Pause for a moment and imagine how many huge campaign decisions—of life and death—were made at these old wooden tables.

KEEP IN MIND Churchill looms large here. You can see his constant props, cigars and whisky, and learn how these vital commodities kept the great man going through the long, busy nights. What you can view is only a third of the extent of the War Rooms; a Churchill Museum, scheduled to open in 2005, will use some of this remaining space to tell more of the story of this remarkable politician and leader, who was also a serious writer.

CAMLEY STREET NATURAL PARK

The humming of cars and clattering of trains just within earshot, a contrast to the tranquil buzzing of tiny creatures and the breezes rustling through the bullrushes, makes you appreciate even more this small nature reserve beside Regent's Canal. A precious haven, it's a great place for a picnic or to spend an hour, and it's close to the British Library (*see #61*) and the British Museum (*see #60*).

Developed on neglected land, the 2-acre park opened in 1985, and the trees, bushes, and walks appear perfectly at home amid their less attractive urban surroundings. There's a choice of short woodland strolls, with little wooded copses good for hide-and-seek or for watching life on the canal or the birds and the bees around you. That's the best thing to do here—encounter nature and discover some really fun facts. The Log Pile has stag beetles, although it's rare to see one, as larvae stay in the wood for seven years before emerging into the wide world. Volunteers are on hand if kids want to launch into activities such as nature detective trails or arts and crafts.

KEEP IN MIND For safe and successful pond dipping, it's best for kids to lie down on the boardwalk; this will help prevent them from falling in. The nature center provides a net for dipping and a small jar for any finds kids wish to examine at the center. To protect yourself and the kids from waterborne diseases, be sure to cover up any cuts before you pond dip, and to wash hands afterward. Another useful tip: don't forget that if you dig too deep, you'll end up fishing out more mud than creatures.

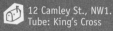 12 Camley St., NW1.
Tube: King's Cross

 Free

M–Th 9–5, Sa–Su 11–5,
or until dusk in winter

020/7833–2311;
www.wildlondon.org

All ages

The best surprise, past the small woodland meadow with its grasses and delicate wildflowers, is the large pond. As you near it, listen for the staccato calls of the coots, which nest in the reed beds surrounding the water's edge. These waterfowl are so tame that they may come up to the boardwalk to greet you briefly before they paddle off again. You might spot one of the stately herons that live in and around the canalside, or even a kingfisher. What you will undoubtedly see in summer are the brightly colored damselflies and dragonflies. In spring, check out the frogs, newts, and toads. Kids can investigate the creatures of the pond more closely with a bit of pond dipping (details from the nature center) from the comfort of the boardwalk, which provides easy access to all the action. If it rains, you can take cover in the informative nature center.

HEY, KIDS! The reason for cutting treetops (coppicing or pollarding, in horticultural language) is not just to make trees more attractive, or to keep them manageable in size. The cutting on top encourages side shoots, which can escape the mouths of hungry deer.

EATS FOR KIDS A short walk away, south of King's Cross station and a five-minute stroll down Mabledon Place opposite the British Library, is the **Valencia** (74 Marchmont St., tel. 020/7713–0269), a good option for sandwiches, snacks, and cappuccino. If you want to picnic in the nature park, you can pick up fixings from one of the many sandwich bars in King's Cross. See also the British Library and the British Museum.

CHANGING OF THE GUARD

57

What photo memories of London are complete without a picture of a stone-faced guard in his black bearskin cap and scarlet tunic, with rifle shouldered? If you want to be snapped with a guard, head to Horse Guards Arch, but for full, foot-stomping pageantry, Buckingham Palace, the Queen's London home, is the place.

In high summer, arrive by 11—10:30 if you want a place by the gates—to stake a good vantage point at the palace. Just before 11:30 you can hear the bands' music, punctuated by shouted commands, as the sea of horses and red tunics winds down Birdcage Walk. It's a great sight, bringing traffic to a stop, and a rousing sound, too, with music from military marches to pop songs. This is the Queen's Guard, made up of the many different regiments of the Household Division, and it's the footguards who "change," or mount sentry. On horseback is the cavalry, the Life Guards or the Blues and Royals, while on foot is a regiment of Grenadiers or Coldstream, Scots, Irish, or Welsh Guards. Among the dazzle of red, gold,

EATS FOR KIDS North of Green Park, a few minutes' walk away, the **Hard Rock Cafe** (150 Old Park La., tel. 020/7629–0382) bulges with rock memorabilia, plays loud music, and does a great business in burgers as well as kids' menus for under-10s.

HEY, KIDS! Originally granted to the Grenadiers for their role in the defeat of Napoleon's army at Waterloo, the furry bearskin cap is surprisingly light. The caps are costly, at around £600, but they can last up to 100 years. Although the Canadian bear pelts are prone to moths and fire, they're preferred to synthetic copies with "fur" that stands alarmingly on end when the wearer is underneath an electricial tower. For more cool guard facts and to view every kind of toy model soldier, visit the Guards Museum (Birdcage Walk, tel. 020/7414–3428), open daily 10-4; there's a small admission charge.

Buckingham Palace and Whitehall, SW1.
Tube: Victoria, St. James's Park

 Free

Buckingham Palace Apr–early Sept,
daily 11:30, check for times in fall and
winter; Horse Guards M–Sa 11, Su 10

020/7839–1377 Buckingham Palace, 020/
7414–2479 Household Division, 09068/
663344 (60p per min); www.visitlondon.com

All ages

and white, you can pick out the different regiments. The Life Guards wear red tunics with white plumed helmets, and the Blues and Royals, blue with red plumed helmets. The Grenadiers' bearskins have white plumes on one side. By day, the soldiers look the historical part in their elaborate dress uniforms, but at night they patrol the palace grounds in combat kit. Occasionally, when the usual guard is on operational duty, you may see the Brigade of Gurkhas or other Commonwealth infantry units.

Other guard mounting takes place daily at Horse Guards Parade, where the Life Guard leaves Hyde Park Barracks via Constitution Hill and The Mall to change duty. At the Tower of the London, you can see the daily Ceremony of the Keys at 10 PM if you obtain a pass in advance from the Tower. You can also spot guard sentries outside St. James's Palace, the offices of the Prince of Wales.

KEEP IN MIND Horse Guards, once Henry VIII's tournament ground (think of the film *A Knight's Tale*), is where the Queen salutes her troops on the second Saturday in June. Tickets for this grand parade, Trooping the Colour, plus the rehearsals, are available in advance by mail from the Household Division. For many royal occasions, the King's Troop, resplendent in black and gold uniforms, fires cannons in Green Park or on Tower Hill. For dates, check with VisitLondon, the tourist board.

CHESSINGTON WORLD OF ADVENTURES

If your kids want their insides thrown out, or at least thoroughly shaken, then the rides at Chessington are for them. This adventure land, 25 miles southwest of London and easily reached by train from Waterloo Station, has something for all age groups and is split into loosely themed zones: Pirate's Cove, Mystic East, Mexicana, Transylvania, Forbidden Kingdom, Toytown, and Animal Land. Since the big thrills attract long lines, arrive early to cut waiting time.

Each ride has a thrillometer star rating, and almost everyone rates Samurai (Mystic East) as terrifyingly tops. Encased in a seat, you hang on for dear life as you are spun around as if on a Japanese warrior's sword. When you regain your G-force, you might move on to Egypt's Forbidden Kingdom for another breathstopper, Rameses Revenge. As the ultimate punishment for disturbing the mummies in the Forbidden Tomb, explorers are treated to a jolly good drenching and a bit of twirling up high. For those who'd rather warm up to the excitement, or for anyone who prefers fractionally less dramatic rides, the Black Buccaneer

HEY, KIDS! Chessington's first incarnation was as a zoo with a couple of rides, and revamped enclosures have helped the animals reclaim a little limelight. The Gorilla Group of one male and six females is one of very few in captivity that has three generations of the same family. Kumba is the big boss at 490 pounds; the smallest is two-year-old Shanga. Come early in the day to see the animals at their most active, or stop by later when they are generally laid back; at any time, you'll get a break from the whirl of screams from the rest of the park.

Chessington, Surrey.
Rail: Chessington South

  From £18 ages 12 and up,
£14.50 children 4-11

Apr-mid-July and early Sept-late Oct,
daily 10-6; mid-July-early Sept and
end of Oct, daily 10-7

0870/444-7777;
www.chessington.com

3 and up

(Pirate's Cove) is ideal: a pirate ship swings back and forth until you are almost horizontal. Another lower-key choice is the Vampire (Transylvania), which takes smaller monsters on board. Scare seekers who prefer to stay grounded can tour Hocus Pocus Hall on foot. Following in the Hogwarts and hobbits vein, this experience features animated wizards and goblins seen through 3-D glasses, as well as some interesting smells that add to the fun.

If you haven't the stomach for all this, or have younger kids in tow, head to Toytown, with its somewhat milder options—although bumping Crazy Cars might not be quite so gentle with excited kids at the wheel. The Safari Skyway takes you over a large section of park, yielding great glimpses of the many wild and exotic beasts in Animal Land, from cute meerkats to prowling tigers. The trip may provide a welcome break from all the adventure.

EATS FOR KIDS
Unless you take a picnic—though in this huge park, carrying extra baggage is a pain—you'll have to rely on one of the many hunger busters: **McDonald's, Pizza Hut, KFC, Mexican Diner,** and **Alpine Café.** Sweet treats can be nibbled on at the **Cadbury Castle.**

KEEP IN MIND Many of the larger, wilder rides have height restrictions for safety, ranging from minimums of 35 inches to 55 inches. On some rides, children must be accompanied by an adult: there's a list on the brochure you get as you enter. Tickets are priced by off-peak, standard, and peak rates (timed with school and bank holidays), not by months, so check ahead to confirm admission charges. Chessington is part of the Tussaud's group and has a (fairly expensive) unlimited admission pass that includes Madame Tussaud's and London Planetarium (see #34) and Warwick Castle.

COURTAULD GALLERY

When it comes to art museums, small is beautiful, especially with children. The compact nature of this gallery is one of its chief assets, making it easy to navigate and manageable for kids, and the setting and many magnificent paintings provide a visual feast.

The prettiest approach to the gallery is from the river, by the steps on Waterloo Bridge, and past the impressive buildings that make up the whole of Somerset House (see #14). Head across the cobbled courtyard to the gallery entrance. The gallery rooms were the first home, from 1780, of the Royal Academy of Arts, which later moved to Burlington House, in Piccadilly, in 1837. If you look up at the decorative plasterwork ceilings, you can still see the curly RA initials. The rooms have had a makeover, but the main reason for coming is to see monumental works by Impressionists and Post-Impressionists.

In order to help kids get the most out of the Courtauld (and enjoy the collection yourself), pick up a children's gallery-trail booklet at the admission desk. These free,

EATS FOR KIDS See Somerset House. A short walk away, the ultimate family entertainment restaurant, **Smollensky's** (105 Strand, tel. 020/7497-2101), has games and magicians. The Tex-Mex-oriented food doesn't quite match up to the class of the art deco interior, but kids have a ball.

KEEP IN MIND You can plunge your kids into the world of painting through free drop-in workshops held the first Saturday of each month (3–5) and during school vacations. These mini master classes allow children to look closely at an artist or style and then produce their own masterpieces—perhaps pastel drawings influenced by Renoir or fabric-pen designs created after looking for textile patterns in paintings. In addition to enriching a young mind, you save money, as one adult per child is admitted free. Separate workshop events during the holidays, for different ages, cost £10–£15 and last four or more hours.

Somerset House, Strand, WC2.
Tube: Covent Garden, Holborn

 020/7848-2526;
www.courtauld.ac.uk

 £5 ages 18 and up; M 10–2
(except holidays) free

 Daily 10–6; last admission 5:15

 5 and up

self-guiding quizzes on a range of themes—best for ages 5–12—turn out to be fun for parents, too. Covering the gallery's key paintings and giving a neat art-history tour, the "Different Kinds of Painting" booklet begins at the beginning. Mariotto Albertinelli's *The Creation and Fall,* an early narrative painting almost 500 years old, spotlights the story of Adam and Eve. The quiz trail then romps through another 100 years to the genius of the Dutch old masters and their portraits and landscapes, before leaping to Impressionists, in the 19th century, and *A Bar at the Folies-Bergère* by Edouard Manet. It's a whistle-stop tour of art styles.

If you'd rather go straight to the Impressionist gems, head up the winding marble staircase. An interested child can spend ages filling out "A Painting for Every Season," another kids' booklet that covers works from Claude Monet's *Autumn Effect at Argenteuil* to *The Haystacks,* by Paul Gauguin. It's not unusual to find yourself stepping over children sprawled on the floor while they draw intently.

HEY, KIDS! The name "Impressionists" was not originally meant to be a compliment. By calling the new style of paintings "impressions," late-19th-century critics were actually mocking them, considering them to be rough and unfinished works rather than proper images. Turning the tables, struggling artists adopted the name for themselves, and the rest is history. Today these "sketchy" paintings, rejected for decades, are admired around the globe, and many sell for millions.

COVENT GARDEN

From its epicenter—the cobbled piazza and its covered market—to the surrounding streets, Covent Garden has trendy shops and eateries galore. Best of all, you can enjoy some of the coolest street shows around. The original "convent garden" was tended by monks in medieval times to provide produce for Westminster Abbey. Markets continued to thrive on the site until steel-and-glass halls were built in the 19th century. Of these, the Jubilee Market (with crafts, cheap fashions, and bric-a-brac), the Floral Hall in the Royal Opera House, and London's Transport Museum (*see #37*), which occupies a former market hall, remain. The restored Central Market has shops, terrace cafés, and a quaint Apple Market with stalls that display beautiful crafts including jewelry, clothes, and toys.

The only building remaining from the square's original 17th-century Italianate design, however, is St. Paul's, the actors' church, whose interior is dotted with great performers' plaques (look for Charlie Chaplin's). In front is *the* street theater hot spot, where mimes line the route to the tube station. You might mistake one for a statue, as a pose can be held for

EATS FOR KIDS Escape the hordes at **Mela** (152–156 Shaftesbury Ave., tel. 020/7836–8635), a bright, modern, Indian restaurant where the food is cooked before your eyes. Choose from flat breads and pancakes (*naan, paratha, dosai*) to roll with spiced vegetables, chicken, and fish, starting at £1.95. The **Vilar Floral Hall Café** (Royal Opera House) is high on spectacle and prices, offering cakes and pastries, sandwiches and salads. The Central Market Hall is cheaper; catch the shopping and entertainment buzz while feasting on huge sandwiches and stuffed potatoes at **Ponti's** (Unit 4, The Market, tel. 020/7836–1662). Also see London's Transport Museum and Theatre Museum.

Covent Garden Piazza and Central Market, WC2.
Tube: Covent Garden

 020/7836–9136 Covent Garden Central
Market; www.coventgardenmarket.co.uk

 Free

 Piazza daily 24 hrs; Jubilee Market Hall M 9–3,
T–Su 9–5; Central Market Hall daily 10–5,
some shops and restaurants much later

All ages

minutes on end. There are global musicians: Chinese players with melodious strings and exotic box instruments or colorful Andean percussion groups. The covered market attracts more musicians, comedians, and contortionists.

The grand old entrance to the Royal Opera House is still on Bow Street, but a massive makeover added a sleek entrance off the piazza. Step inside and enjoy the new spaces, particularly the restored Floral Hall, formerly a storeroom for stage props and, before that, a 19th-century flower market. Now it's a public area where you can eat snacks while gazing up at the glass ceiling and also admire displays of vintage spangled ballet costumes. An escalator takes you to the Vilar Floral Hall Bar and an outdoor balcony with a magnificent view across the market rooftops to Nelson's Column and the tourists in Trafalgar Square. Rehearsal rooms for the Royal Ballet have windows onto the balcony; if you're lucky, you might glimpse a young star.

KEEP IN MIND
London's Transport Museum and Theatre Museum (see #37 and #9) are next to the piazza. Across Long Acre, and to the left of Neal Street, is Neal's Yard, a mock rustic courtyard with whole-food shops and eating places and a quirky water clock that performs hourly.

HEY, KIDS! Street theater, including puppetry, has been a tradition here for centuries. In 1662, the great diarist Samuel Pepys noted that he had enjoyed an Italian puppet play here—the best he ever saw, and probably the first Mr. Punch show. For over 25 years, the annual May Fayre has celebrated this theatrical event in the garden of St. Paul's, where over 30 gaily striped Punch-and-Judy booths stage performances on the second Sunday in May. It's wonderful free entertainment and a great chance to enjoy a British seaside and fairground tradition (tel. 020/7375–0441 for more information). You can try making your own puppet, too.

CUTTY SARK

Walk the decks of this beautiful ship, and you'll be taking a step into the past. The last of the clippers that sailed the seas to bring back tea and spices from China, the *Cutty Sark* is resplendent with masts and rigging and is one of the London riverside's most famous historic sights. As you board, breathe in a little of the smoky aroma of Lapsang souchong tea absorbed over the years.

The history of the ship, launched in 1869, is told in storyboards, with captions especially for kids at the base of each board. In its glory days, the *Cutty Sark* (Scots for "cut short") sliced through the seas and set record journey times to the other side of the world. When her cargo changed from tea to wool and thus her route from China to South Australia, she could dash off the voyage in just 77 days, overtaking the mail steamship.

On the deck below, find out if you pass muster as a sailor by pulling some of the weighted blocks and tackles for hoisting the sails, but first feel the strength of the sail section

HEY, KIDS!

Captain Woodget was one of the *Cutty Sark*'s most celebrated bosses, respected by all who worked with him. To relax, he bicycled on deck with his three dogs following behind. Check out the photo of him and his pets in the exhibit on the ship's history.

EATS FOR KIDS Follow the seafaring theme at the wood-paneled, 18th-century **Trafalgar Tavern** (Park Row, tel. 020/8858–2437). It was a favorite haunt of Charles Dickens and of government ministers who would travel downriver from Westminster to feast on the specialty whitebait (a tiny white fish), which was caught locally. Children's options in the restaurant include bangers and mash (sausage and mashed potatoes), fish sticks, and chicken nuggets. **Café Rouge** (30 Stockwell St., tel. 020/8293–6660) serves French-style burgers and fries. Also see Greenwich Park, National Maritime Museum, and Royal Observatory.

King William Walk, Greenwich, SE10.
Tube: Cutty Sark

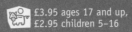 £3.95 ages 17 and up,
£2.95 children 5–16

 Daily 10–5; last entry ½ hr
before closing

 020/8858–3445;
www.cuttysark.org.uk

4 and up

by the stairs. Then imagine it being wet from storm and spray, increasing its weight many times over. Rope knotting was a necessary skill. It's amazing how many types of knots there are to learn, each with a purpose. (On weekends and in summer, there are knot demonstrations by a real salty dog sailor.) To rest your weary bones, try getting in a hammock, but mind your balance lest you fall.

Above deck, officers' and crew accommodations have been restored to their original condition—all shiny wood and authentic fittings. The captain's saloon is the most luxurious; note the hanging tray that holds wineglasses secure. For the rest of the crew, accommodations are spare, as you can see by peering in on some of the waxwork crew at ease in their quarters. Above deck is a wonderful web of rigging that totals 11 miles— such a romantic sight when set against the towers of the city in the distance.

KEEP IN MIND Wear sensible shoes to negotiate the many steep, narrow steps. You'll also be suitably attired to wander around the winding village streets and the covered Greenwich Market on College Approach (it sells crafts, antiques, and tasty things to eat), or to explore part of the Thames Path, which has great riverside views. Allow a full day in Greenwich, as there's much to see, including Greenwich Park, the National Maritime Museum, and the Royal Observatory (*see #50, #26, and #18*). The tourist information center by the *Cutty Sark* is a useful starting point for orienting your day.

FIREPOWER

Guns, tanks, and plenty more can be seen—and heard, with accompanying booms and bangs—at the Royal Artillery's museum, just a little downriver from Greenwich. Complete with atmospheric effects, Firepower provides an engaging experience of history, as you explore the life and role of the gunner. Just to walk around the exterior of the Royal Arsenal's regal buildings, such as the Military Academy and Gunnery Hall, gives a powerful sense of the importance of the arsenal over 300 years. This is where guns and munitions were made to guard the British empire.

As you wait to enter the Field of Fire, you can discover the beginnings of artillery, with the Board of Ordnance, and the first foundry (which moved here from Moorfields) for making cannon. Step into the Field of Fire, with its background of archival and new film projected all around, and you are thrust into the maelstrom of battle. The floor vibrates, lights flash, and smoke hangs in the air; through the bangs, the tragic and triumphant stories and reports of combat are told by gunners who were in the thick of battle, from the Somme in World

KEEP IN MIND The Royal Arsenal and dockyards at Woolwich have only recently been developed, and the area is gaining popularity with visitors. If you want to arrive by river, the station at North Woolwich has a ferry connection from the north bank. As you travel, you can imagine the glorious scene here when Elizabeth I met Sir Francis Drake on his return from navigating the world's seas and knighted him on his ship, the *Golden Hinde* (see #51). The views by the river are quite open and spacious, as you are en route east to the county of Kent.

Royal Arsenal, Woolwich, SE 18. Rail: Woolwich
Arsenal (from Charing Cross or London Bridge).
Tube: North Greenwich, then Bus 161, 422, or 472

£6.50 ages 17 and up,
£4.50 children 5–16,
£18 family

Su–W 10–5:30; school
vacations daily 10:30–5

020/8855–7755; www.firepower.org.uk

7 and up

War I to the Gulf War in 1991. After learning about their personal experiences, you may feel a little more informed as you view the weaponry and read other stories in the museum. In the Medals Gallery, you'll see that gunners have been awarded the most Victoria Crosses—Britain's highest award for bravery.

There's plenty of opportunity for fun and skill, too, with pointing and "shooting" galore in interactive games. The games do teach one serious point: being on target and being quick to reload might keep you alive in battle. Also on display are tanks and guns—some with battle scars, and many with touch-screen storyboards so kids can investigate the facts and technology behind the weaponry. In the History Gallery, you can see the progression from Chinese gunpowder, stone catapults, and exploding cannonballs to rockets and missiles—basically, whatever it took to blast out the enemy.

EATS FOR KIDS

You're off the beaten track here, so take advantage of the museum **Café** and its hot and cold snacks such as jacket potatoes (potatoes baked in their skins) with different toppings, and sandwiches and drinks. If you arrived via Greenwich, there are many choices there.

HEY, KIDS! Look for the report of a local boy, Gunner Albert Smith, who received his Victoria Cross medal for heroic deeds in the Nile campaign in 1885. Despite his own knife wounds, Smith held out against the dervish tribesmen. Perhaps later on he watched the football (soccer) matches of the Arsenal team, formed by the armament workers, on Plumstead Common. After winning all the titles around, the "Gunners'" team moved north of the river to Highbury in 1913, much to the annoyance of the nearby club, Tottenham. Today their very competitive matches are explosive.

GOLDEN HINDE

Get on board, me hearties! After circumnavigating the globe and sailing more than 140,000 miles, the *Golden Hinde* has come to rest along the Thames. The galleon on the South Bank is not the famous 16th-century man-of-war captained by Sir Francis Drake, however. That one rotted long ago. Instead, a beautiful handcrafted replica, docked between Southwark Cathedral and Shakespeare's Globe *(see #15)*, acts as a living museum. When at sea, its small crew lives exactly as Drake's men did. Life was hard, and the men were tough, as you'll discover on this virtual voyage into the past.

The information sheet for a self-guided tour details the parts of the ship and helps you sort out the mizzen from the mainmast and foremast. Better still is a tour with guides in period dress (book ahead). Either way, between the masts and the bowels of the ship, you can explore five decks. The poop deck, for instance, held the only private cabin—the captain's. (The crew slept among pigs, chickens, and sheep, which were kept for food.) In the main deck's armory, you can try turning the capstan to haul the anchor. On the gun deck

EATS FOR KIDS You need go no farther than the **Old Thameside Inn** (St. Mary Overie Dock, tel. 020/7403–4243), opposite the ship, for lunchtime sandwiches and salads. Actually a converted dock warehouse, it has views over the river that can't be beat.

KEEP IN MIND The *Golden Hinde* is run by a small outfit that relies on admission fees, so you may have to be patient when reserving a tour (£3.50 adults, £2.50 children). You can also book a living-history night, during which your family (adults must accompany children) can dress, sleep, eat, and work as part of Drake's crew. It's an unforgettable experience. If you can't stay for the night, you might want to try one of the daytime summer workshops, offered when school is out. Call for details.

St Mary Overie Dock, Cathedral St., SE1.
Tube: London Bridge

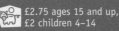 £2.75 ages 15 and up,
£2 children 4–14

Daily; times vary

0870/011–8700;
www.goldenhinde.co.uk

 6 and up

(painted red to camouflage bloodstains), you may get a chance to load the cannon and see it fire. By the way, if a lowly shipmate was found somewhere he shouldn't have been, punishment was severe. If he stole food, for example, his hand was nailed to the mast; after a few hours, the hand would probably have had to be chopped off. Among Drake's crew of musicians, cook, blacksmith, and minister, there was a barber surgeon, who performed amputations—with only alcohol as painkiller.

Watch your head while descending the ladders to the lower decks; headroom is minimal to keep the boat's center of gravity low. Here you'll find the bilge, where rocks stabilized the ship; food-storage barrels; and the galley, where meals—including salted and dried beef, beans, prunes, currants, and sea biscuits, often with maggots and other creepy crawlies—were prepared. Food for thought: with all this, how were Drake's men so victorious in battle?

HEY, KIDS! Young boys on the crew worked hard. One of their tasks was to carry the gunpowder for the guns. The boys were called powder monkeys because they climbed up and down the ladders from the lower deck to the gun deck as fast as their bent, monkeylike legs could carry them. When off duty, powder monkeys slept on the deck floor (with mouths shut to prevent animal waste from sloshing into their mouths!) in the same set of ragged clothes.

GREENWICH PARK

Flanked by the River Thames, Greenwich is the oldest royal park. Henry VIII hunted in the 183-acre park, and he and his daughters, Mary and Elizabeth, were born in Greenwich Palace. The palace was eventually demolished, and the great architects Christopher Wren and John Vanbrugh built the Royal Naval Hospital for Queen Mary, to rival Wren's Royal Hospital in Chelsea. It later became the Royal Naval College. These grand buildings on the river, which include two domed structures with an open court between them, set the tone for a historical walk across the park.

St. Mary's Gate, by the *Cutty Sark,* is a good place to start, as it takes you directly along the Avenue to the heart and highest point of the park. From here you can take in the park's most beautiful panorama—on a clear day you see across to St. Paul's Cathedral and the modern blocks of the Docklands. No wonder, then, that at 155 feet above sea level, this was the place of choice for the Royal Observatory (*see #18*), also built by Wren. The observatory is home to the Meridian line, and you can stand with your feet astride the point where

EATS FOR KIDS There are many cafés in the park, but the most popular is the **Park Café** (Great Cross Ave., tel. 020/8858–9695), by the Royal Observatory. Sit at the outdoor tables and order breakfast (all day), burgers, or baked potatoes with toppings. The park is perfect for a picnic on a fine day; buy picnic fare in Greenwich village from **M&S Simply Food** store (55–57 Greenwich Church St., tel. 020/8858–6704). Also see *Cutty Sark,* National Maritime Museum, and Royal Observatory.

King William Walk,
Greenwich, SE10.
Tube: Cutty Sark

020/8858–2608;
www.royalparks.gov.uk

Free

Daily sunrise–sunset

All ages

east meets west, just as everyone else does. Luckily, cars aren't allowed on this road between 10 and 4, so you can take photos in safety. The hill is great for rolling, running, or (in snow) sledding down. A somber statue of General Wolfe, who won a victory in Québec that added Canada to the British empire, towers over the scene.

Having gone up the hill, you might return to the riverside or else explore one of the many tree-lined avenues leading to gardens. The Flower Garden by the lake is a riot of color, scents, and butterflies in spring and summer. In spring, the Dell is magical; finches dart in and out of rhododendrons, and if you are very quiet in the Wilderness, you may spot the shy deer that have bred here for centuries. For kids who'd rather jump, climb, and make loads of noise, a playground by Park Row Gate has enough apparatus to keep them happy for an hour or more.

HEY, KIDS! At Elizabeth's Oak, the queen took tea in a hollow tree almost 6 feet across, which later became a tiny prison for people who broke park rules. You can also find what might be the remains of a Roman temple at the far end of Lovers' Walk.

KEEP IN MIND Getting here is part of the fun. Boats depart from Westminster Pier and pass the Tower of London during the scenic 35-minute ride to Greenwich. By train, the elevated Docklands Light Rail line runs through the ultra-modern Docklands. If you get out at the Island Gardens station, you can walk to Greenwich underneath the river. Built in 1902 to replace a 300-year-old ferry, the foot tunnel is found near the *Cutty Sark*. At its maximum depth, it is 53 feet beneath the river, and the tunnel is just under ¼ mile long. It echoes eerily, but the atmosphere is neat.

HAMPSTEAD HEATH

Covering almost 800 acres, with beautiful views, Hampstead Heath is a great open space flanked by the historic north London villages of Hampstead and Highgate with their Georgian terraced houses. Today everyone comes to relax or to walk, jog, picnic, fly kites, rollerblade, or cycle. In earlier times, the heath was a wild place, and washerwomen would use the ponds and hang the clothes of the rich and posh on the still-common prickly yellow gorse bushes.

The south end of the heath is the most appealing for kids because of its playgrounds and pool. You can get here easily from the station, beyond Nassington Road. Head to the Information Centre for a free map, and while you choose a route (guided walks are available), kids can explore the heath's history and wildlife through a touch and smell exhibit and a computer program. An outdoor pool (admission charged) is beside the center; a free wading pool for smaller kids is between the jungle-style adventure play area and a more traditional playground.

HEY, KIDS!

Parliament Hill (known as Kite Hill) got its name because it was from here that Guy Fawkes and his gang, who tried to blow up Parliament in 1605, hoped to view their handiwork. Though their attempt was foiled, their plot is celebrated with fireworks every November 5.

EATS FOR KIDS

A **café** (tel. 020/7485–6606) at the foot of Parliament Hill dishes up daily Italian specials along with salads, snacks, cakes, and drinks. By the tube and train stations, in central and south Hampstead, there are numerous coffee shops, pizzerias, and burger joints. A quick, fun option, the cheap and cheerful **Hampstead Creperie** (77 Hampstead High St., tel.020/7372–0081) prepares sweet and savory pancakes before your eyes in a mobile cart.

South End Rd., Hampstead, NW3. Silverlink rail: Hampstead Heath, from Highbury and Islington. Bus: 24, 46, 168, C11

 Free

020/7482-7073; www.cityoflondon.gov.uk/openspaces

 Heath daily 24 hrs; information center Mar–Oct, W–F 1–5, Sa–Su 10–5; Nov–Feb, W–F 1–4, Sa–Su 10–4; pool May–Sept, daily 7–7

All ages

To walk on the wilder side, set off west to the highest point of the heath, Parliament Hill. On weekends it's often topped with colorful flying kites. There's a wonderful view of London way below. A walk eastward takes you to the ponds, noisy with ducks and model boats, and behind hedges are segregated ponds for women and men. The free ponds make a refreshing experience—if you don't mind sharing the water with waterfowl and creepy crawlies. In summer, the coed pond at the foot of East Heath is popular. On spring and summer bank holiday weekends (a Monday closure creates a long weekend), East Heath has traditionally hosted a fun fair.

Beyond the tame attractions, you can discover the heath's natural beauty on trails ranging from 2 to 6 miles. Through woodland, wetland, and grassland, you can spot many bird species; bat walks are sometimes scheduled at night. On your return journey on a dusky summer evening, you might just catch a glimpse of a fox, rabbit, or deer.

KEEP IN MIND The suggested route covers a small section of the heath, skirting East Heath and Parliament Hill, north and east of Hampstead village, although even this could take a meandering three hours. To see another beautiful part of the heath, near Highgate, visit the area around Kenwood House (see #43). If you have kids with limited stamina, visit the heath in microcosm at Golders Hill Park. There's a playground, bandstand, and animal enclosure with deer and goats, and an aviary with flamingos and other birds—all free. A bit north of Hampstead proper, Golders Green is the nearest tube.

HAMPTON COURT PALACE

Along with wives, King Henry VIII couldn't resist collecting palaces, of which Hampton Court was the most magnificent. Sitting beside the Thames in acres of parkland, it's a wonderful place to explore. Taking a boat from Richmond is the most panoramic way to arrive, but the trip takes almost two hours. You should allow at least four hours at the palace to make the most of your visit.

The vast palace holds 500 years of royal history, and royal treasures from the 1700s on fill the state apartments. Standing in the cobbled courtyard entrance, you are catapulted back to the 1700s, as gentlemen of King William's court, in their lacy finery, are ready to escort you on a free tour. If you prefer to make your own way round, some excellent quiz sheets form an investigative trail that's good for children 11 and under. The themes include eerie ghostly stories, a history of the Tudor era, and fascinating feasts. The Tudor Kitchens are the most engrossing area of the palace for all ages, but the dishes aren't for the modern palate ("gross" is the usual response). The butcher's room has splattered blood and holly

EATS FOR KIDS Choose between the **Tiltyard Tearoom,** which is set among the rose and herbaceous gardens and has a wide-ranging menu of hot and cold food and kids' lunch boxes (around £3) and the smaller **Privy Kitchen Coffee Shop,** with lighter snack alternatives. You are also welcome to eat on the outdoor patio and to bring your own picnic (although picnickers are not encouraged in the formal gardens). If you don't arrive with your own food, you can pick something up at the grocery stores in nearby Hampton village.

East Molesey, Surrey.
Rail: Hampton Court

 0870/753-7777,
1865/324120 outside
the U.K.; www.hrp.org.uk

 £11.50 ages 16 and up, £7.50
children 5–15; maze £2.30
ages 16 and up, £1.50 children;
grounds free

 Mar–Oct, M 10:15–6, T–Su 9:30–6; Nov–Mar,
daily 9:30–4:30; grounds daily 7 AM–dusk;
last entry 45 mins before closing

 5 and up

sprigs for cleaning the tables. In the hanging room you can peer in to see the game—swan, peacock, and boar; in the kitchen you can crush sage with mortar and pestle and try lifting the massive pots. Tables are laid with replicas, such as fish and deer pies. Over the roaring fire, a cauldron bubbles with soup, which you may be able to taste. Note the stool where a young boy would turn a spit with pig or boar. Feasting was serious stuff, and cooking was a hot, laborious business.

More than 60 acres of beautiful park and gardens surround the palace. Children run around fountains and play in the Wilderness section, which includes Hampton Court's treasure: a large, impressive hedged maze. Kids (and adults) love wandering back and forth, hitting the same dead ends time and again. Wise parents sit outside, listen to their kids' delighted screams of frustration, and enjoy the tranquillity of the gardens.

HEY, KIDS! Henry VIII didn't have Hampton Court built; he basically stole it. Its previous owner, Cardinal Wolsey, was becoming a little too big for his boots, and Henry wanted the palace for himself. So on the pretext of using it for a grand meeting that lasted a long time, Henry took it over and simply didn't hand it back.

KEEP IN MIND Throughout the year—generally during school and bank holiday vacations—Hampton Court has special free programs, including little dramas performed by actors in period costume. You might be asked to take part, perhaps joining in some Tudor dancing, or you can follow a little swordplay or watch a falcon display. Ask at the Information Centre in the Clock Court, or phone ahead. If you're also planning to visit the Tower of London (see #6), check out money-saving joint tickets for the two sights.

HAWK CONSERVANCY

Come by train (just over an hour from Waterloo Station) or by car (via the M3 and A303), but come. Even those with only a passing interest in raptors (birds of prey) will leave charmed and very much the wiser. You'll see birds native to the British Isles and from as far away as South America (most in captive breeding programs), from large condors to the small pygmy owl. You'll learn the difference between eagles, falcons, and hawks, and you might even develop a sneaking respect for vultures, those bottom-of-the-heap, bad-boy-image birds. Most birds are viewed in caged natural settings amid a small wooded park area surrounded by unspoiled woodland, but when the raptors come out to play, watch out.

Three daily demonstrations display the birds' talents. At the top flying field (large bird displays), you may want to duck as kites swoop from every direction, niftily catching food in flight. Meanwhile, a keeper tells all you need to know about these graceful flyers and happily answers questions almost endlessly afterward. (The conservancy was started by a nature-loving husband-and-wife team, and that caring family atmosphere is still very much

KEEP IN MIND Make sure to arrive before noon, when the first of the major flying displays takes place, followed by others at 2 and 3:30. The displays, along with most of the attractions, are in the open air, so don't forget to bring cover for rain showers.

HEY, KIDS! Not all the birds at the conservancy are captive. At the sound of a bell each afternoon at the wildflower meadow, many beautiful wild birds—herons and some-times kites and other raptors that have been released back into the wild—come to feed. You can watch this wonderful scene undercover in the bird blind—but hush, or you'll scare them away.

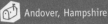 Andover, Hampshire

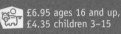 £6.95 ages 16 and up, £4.35 children 3–15

Mid-Feb–Oct, daily 10:30–5:30

01264/773850 voice, 01264/772252 recording; www.hawk-conservancy.org

5 and up

in evidence.) The lower flying field features the fun and games of Chestnut, the tawny owl, and a mischievous kestrel. Undoubtedly, the most thrilling display is at the Valley of the Eagles, where three majestic bald eagles fly from a far field—you can just make them out as specks in the distance—to the display area, perfectly in time to dramatic music.

Between demonstrations, try wearing a special glove, steadying your nerves, and launching a Harris hawk into flight—not as easy as it looks. Stop along the leafy walkways and gaze at countless beautiful birds, particularly the elegant secretary bird and the many cute, wide-eyed owls. Don't forget to say a special hello to Duffy the eagle owl, with perky feathered ears; he's been around so long he practically owns the place. And why not place bets on the furry but feather-free ferrets, who run riot to raise funds for the hawk hospital?

EATS FOR KIDS The conservancy is deep in the countryside, so unless you have brought a picnic, you'll have to eat at **Duffy's,** named for the conservancy's star eagle owl. It serves a range of child-friendly meals and snacks, such as sausages, burgers, and fries, but not a raw chicken leg in sight, as these treats are reserved for the raptors.

HMS BELFAST

Kids—young boys especially—love clambering on the big guns of this warship, launched in 1938 and today Europe's last World War II survivor. In a fantastic South Bank location—on the Thames, in the shadow of the Tower of London—it provides a fun way to discover more about wartime history and about life on board ship, from the quarterdeck to the engine room. You'll find plenty to see, from gun shells to ship's rations, and there are also videos and interactive games, so allow up to two hours.

The ship is divided into eight zones, and kids can follow their own self-guided trail. If you visit during school vacations, there are extra quiz trails and the occasional interactive drama. Apart from the guns, the captain's bridge is a definite hot spot. Here you get a taste of what it was like to command this huge vessel in a red alert. Lifelike models and frenetic voice recordings re-create what the crew of the *Belfast* encountered against the German battle cruiser *Scharnhorst* (one of the enemy's largest warships) at the Battle of North Cape. The boiler and engine rooms down below are massive, necessary to drive this great

EATS FOR KIDS The onboard **Walrus Café** is so called because of the tiny Walrus seaplanes that used to be stored here. Kids can admire the rivet- and pipe-lined walls while digging into a children's lunch box of sandwich, fruit, muffin, and drink (£4.50). A short walk away toward Waterloo Station, Gabriel's Wharf has a larger selection of eateries, including the **Gourmet Pizza Company** (tel. 020/7928–3188). The many wonderful pizza variations are big on creative toppings, and a boardwalk patio overlooks the river. See also BFI London Imax Cinema and the Tower of London.

Morgan's Lane, Tooley St., SE1.
Tube: London Bridge

 £6 ages 17 and up.
Children 16 and under free

 Mar–Oct, daily 10–6; Nov–Feb,
daily 10–5; last entry 45 mins
before closing

020/7940–6300;
www.iwm.org.uk

5 and up

warhorse, which, at full steam, ran at 80,000 horsepower. On other decks, you'll learn about the hard life of ordinary seamen, rum rations notwithstanding. (While serving for two years in the Far East, the crew washed down 56,000 pints of Navy rum.)

Augmenting the experience, videos show reenactments of the ship's heroic engagements, explain how important areas of the ship worked, and demonstrate what had to be done to make the ship watertight if a shell hit. On D-Day in June 1944, when the Allies landed on the Normandy beaches, HMS *Belfast* played a vital part in transporting and protecting the troops. Operation Neptune, the naval part of the landing—depicted in the opening sequence of the movie *Saving Private Ryan*—was a crucial turning point in the history of the war, and the *Belfast* remains to help tell the tale.

KEEP IN MIND
The decks are linked by steep, ladderlike stairs, so wear comfortable shoes with nonslip soles. After your visit, stroll downriver across Tower Bridge for a view of the *Belfast*. The river path westward, the Millennium Mile, goes past the Millennium Bridge (*see #33*) to the London Eye.

HEY, KIDS! Each of the HMS *Belfast*'s triple, 175-ton guns had a range of 14 miles. Currently the turrets are trained northward on a service station on the M1 motorway, or highway. If you enjoyed this visit, you might want to check out more hands-on marine hardware in the Submarine exhibit at the Imperial War Museum (*see #45*), where you can swing through a submarine hatch and take control of a dive.

IMPERIAL WAR MUSEUM

45

The enormous guns flanking the entrance might suggest that this massive museum on the South Bank is merely a glorified showcase for war making, but it's far more than that. In addition to housing exhibits on 20th-century war tactics and machinery, it chronicles the human side of wartime—fear, bravery, and the spirit of camaraderie.

The impressive hardware on display includes howitzers, armored cars, a German one-man submarine, a Lancaster bomber, a V2 rocket, and a bomber you can get inside. Among the numerous hands-on exhibits are the huge periscope that focuses as far as St. Paul's Cathedral and the Submarine section, where you can clamber inside and take the controls.

Other exhibits focus on life during wartime. Away from the front lines, the focus is on women's fashions and food, and poetry and art reveal emotion in the heat of battle. The Blitz Experience gives a taste of London during the German air bombardment of World War II. In a reconstructed air-raid shelter on a 1940 street, you smell acrid smoke; hear sirens, fire-

HEY, KIDS!

In wartime Britain, food was rationed. Can you imagine having to eat powdered everything, from milk to eggs, and margarine in tins? You were allowed just a handful of sweets and very few goodies each week. Check out a typical weekly grocery ration in the Home Front, in the World War II section.

KEEP IN MIND A testament to the millions of lives that were lost, the Holocaust Exhibition documents the persecution of the Jews and other minority groups in World War II, giving the personal stories behind the everyday objects, letters, and photographs. The exhibit can produce powerful emotions and might be distressing for younger children. Kids who want to find out about the uniforms and battles of earlier centuries should march around to the National Army Museum (Royal Hospital Rd., Chelsea, tel. 020/7730–0717).

engine bells, and the bombs themselves; and imagine fearing your home has been destroyed. The Trench, a reconstruction of the Somme, France, in 1916, shows the ghastliness of World War I trench warfare. Lighting, sounds, and smells re-create what a "tommy" soldier endured, from trench foot (rot from constantly standing in mud and water) to the horror of climbing out of the trench into a barrage of gunfire.

The role of secrets is touched upon, too. On the ground floor you can decipher some Morse code, while on the first floor, an espionage and intelligence section has invisible ink and the Enigma cipher machine. Interactive videos cover famous intelligence operations and conflicts, such as the siege of London's Iranian embassy in 1980. Bringing the museum to life, Gallery Adventures are free kids' programs that run alongside special exhibitions (there are also events during school vacations). They include enactments of landmark events, such as the great POW escapes from Colditz Castle. It all adds up to an amazing amount to see; one visit is hardly enough.

EATS FOR KIDS Thankfully, **The Café** is a ration-free zone. It serves freshly prepared hot and cold meals, kids' meals, and lunchboxes with a sandwich, fruit drink, cake, and fruit. Those who bring their own lunch can eat in a picnic room on the lower ground floor or outside in the gardens around the museum if the weather's fine. Good supplies can be found at sandwich shops in nearby Kennington Road.

KENSINGTON GARDENS

Of all the London parks, Kensington Gardens is essentially the children's park, with its Peter Pan connections, wide open spaces, boating lake, and the latest addition, the Princess Diana Memorial Playground. It was the princess who put Kensington on the map—and in the world's newspapers—and was probably the most famous resident of Kensington Palace, situated on the edge of the park.

Although Kensington Gardens seems to merge into Hyde Park, the Long Water, which leads into the Serpentine boating lake, separates the two spaces. William III chose the fresh air and peaceful green fields of Kensington for his family home, and more than 300 years later, the park still has that rambling, wild feel, far from the noise of busy Bayswater Road to the north and Kensington Gore to the south. There are tranquil, formal gardens with fountains and paths to run around in the elegant Italian Gardens, to the north of the Long Water, near Lancaster Gate. The long Flower Walk, at the opposite end of the park, is a joy, with pretty displays to admire throughout the year. Along the Long Water, a bronze Peter Pan

Bordered by Bayswater Rd., Long Water, Kensington Gore, Kensington Palace Gardens. Tube: High Street Kensington, Lancaster Gate, Queensway

 Free

 Daily sunrise–sunset

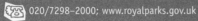 020/7298–2000; www.royalparks.gov.uk

All ages

statue is set in an enchanted woodland area, where kids can hide behind bushes. He plays his pipe to fairies and rabbits, which appear to pop out almost magically from the gnarled, treelike base of the statue. To the west of this is the Round Pond, where children sail toy boats and swans glide; if you're here when daylight fades, you may see bats flitting over the water.

The Princess Diana Memorial Playground, near the Black Lion Gate park entrance and the Queensgate tube, explores the Peter Pan theme even further, with beautiful wood equipment amid the grass. Children can climb and swashbuckle away thanks to a pirate galleon, wigwams, and a magical fountain. Don't miss the old Elfin Oak by the playground. Sculpted in the bark of the slightly hollowed stump, fairies, elves, and woodland animals look as if they could be charmed to life after dusk, when the visitors have gone home.

KEEP IN MIND

You can see 18th-century state rooms at Kensington Palace (tel. 0870/751–5180), where some of the royals still live. The palce also contains the formal royal dress collection. It's open daily 10–5; cost is £10.20 adults, £6.60 kids 15 and under (family ticket £31).

HEY, KIDS! The creator of Peter Pan, Sir James Barrie, lived just a short walk away from Kensington Gardens at 100 Bayswater Road (look for the Blue Plaque on the house). It was on his many walks through the park that he met the Llewellyn-Davies boys, who were the inspiration for the Darling family and their adventures in Never Land. A writer and dramatist, Barrie has been practically immortalized himself for the 1904 play that has overshadowed his other works. He is reported to have said, "Some of my plays peter out, and some pan out."

KENWOOD HOUSE

On the edge of Hampstead Heath, between the two charming old London villages of Hampstead and Highgate, lies Kenwood House. The reasons to visit it are many: you can tour the magnificent mansion, along the way seeing some wonderful paintings by the old masters. You can stroll its landscaped woodland gardens, or you can mount the high covered viewing stand just outside the grounds for a great view of the green space that survives so close to the city, and then continue with a walk on the heath.

As befits a mansion built by Robert Adam in 1764 for the Lord Chancellor, Lord Mansfield, the house has sumptuous rooms. Of them, the library is in a league of its own, with classic, templelike ceiling decorations and columns that astound and amaze. Kids might prefer the paintings, however, including some of the world's most famous. *The Guitar Player*, by Vermeer; a Rembrandt self-portrait; and *The Man with a Cane*, by Frans Hals, are included in a children's activity leaflet that explains the house's history and highlights and prompts kids to write and draw their impressions and findings. Kids might also like the

KEEP IN MIND To get information on the Lakeside Concerts (July–August), call Ticketmaster (0870/333–6206) or Ticketselect (0870/890–0146), or check the English Heritage Web site. Concerts start in the early evening; music ranges from classic to jazz and show tunes. Bring a blanket and a picnic.

EATS FOR KIDS Kenwood's **Brew House** (note the Guinness connection), in the spacious white stable and coach house, is a family restaurant that, on weekends and during school vacations, serves kids' favorites such as macaroni and cheese, chicken, sausages, and salmon. Pastries and cakes make a scrumptious dessert. Walking back to Hampstead, you'll find **Spaniards Inn** (Spaniards Rd., tel. 020/8731–6571), a historic tollgate pub with a pretty garden, paneled interior, log fires, and hot dishes of the day. The notorious highwayman Dick Turpin, gentleman painter Joshua Reynolds, and the poet Shelley all rested here.

Hampstead La., NW3. Tube: Archway or Golders Green, then Bus 210

 Free

020/8348–1286; www.english-heritage.org.uk

 House Easter–Aug, Sa–Tu, Th 10–6; W, F 10:30–6; Sept–Nov and Dec–Easter, Sa–Tu, Th 10–4; W, F 10:30–4. Gardens daily, dawn–dusk

 All ages

charming portraits of children, including one of the duke of Wellington's goddaughter; *Miss Murray*, by Thomas Lawrence; and Joseph Wright's exquisitely lit *Dressing the Kitten*, as well as some gorgeous Thomas Gainsborough society ladies. Tucked away upstairs is a curious collection of shoe buckles—the sparkly ones would make hot fashion today.

Kenwood's gardens, its other great treasure, lead down to a lake with ducks and other waterbirds. In summer, this is the scene of outdoor evening concerts, many of which end in spectacular firework displays. If you time your visit to coincide with an afternoon pre-concert rehearsal, you can picnic or throw a Frisbee with musical accompaniment. In late spring, the rhododendrons and azaleas near the house are ablaze with color; this is a great place for chasing and playing hide-and-seek, as is the ivy tunnel. Another, almost-secret spot is the enclosed Kitchen Gardens; you can jump from step to step on the sundial while telling the time. Just don't be in a hurry to leave.

HEY, KIDS! Edward Guinness, the first earl of Iveagh, bought Kenwood to house his paintings in 1924, and in 1927 bequeathed the collection to the nation. (This generous earl also set up houses in the poorer parts of London for people who couldn't afford other places to live.) The Guinness family wealth came from the now well-known brewing business. The beer that bears the family name is the black brew known as stout, which has its roots in Ireland, although it is brewed worldwide today.

KEW BRIDGE STEAM MUSEUM

This fascinating little museum is known worldwide for its Cornish beam engines, housed in a former Victorian pumping station with a tall standpipe tower. Each weekend, these terrific engines are cranked up by a team of enthusiasts, who also love to answer questions about how these humongous pieces of machinery pumped out water.

This particular pumping station supplied west London for over a century, and the steam hall once housed six boilers. Three-level walkways enable you to appreciate the beasts' full size, and the operating machines let you experience a slightly steamy atmosphere. Now imagine a time when all the boilers were fired up and a team of brawny men hand-shoveled coal. This is a good trip for any kid who likes to see how things work, but the brightly painted beams, pumps, pistons, and flywheels—living sculptures that sing, hiss, and sigh with steam—also appeal to kids who just like to look at cool stuff. The engines have romantic names and interesting stories. Dancers End Twin Beam used to pump water to Lord Rothschild's country estate. The Grand Junction 90-incher, one of the Cornish beam engines

EATS FOR KIDS Only open on weekends noon–2, the **Babcock Café,** in the old boiler room (Babcock was a Victorian engineer), serves lunchtime food that is far from old or boiled. You might find baked salmon, chicken curry, or vegetarian bakes, plus a soup of the day and sandwiches, on the daily changing menu. Main meals begin at £4, and smaller kids' portions are available. On weekdays, bring a picnic and eat in the steam hall or by the waterwheel outside if the weather is fine.

Green Dragon La., Brentford.
Rail: Kew Bridge via Waterloo.
Tube: Gunnersbury, then Bus 237 or 267

 020/8568-4757; www.kbsm.org

 M–F £4 ages 16 and up, £2 children 5–15, £10 family ticket; Sa–Su £5.20 ages 16 and up, £3 children, £15.95 family. Free after 4.

Daily 11–5

8 and up

that originally pumped here, is the largest 20-ton working engine of its type in the world (in action 3–3:30 weekends). At full tilt it delivered 472 gallons per stroke. A larger Cornish engine (a 100-incher not back in working order yet) pumped 717 gallons per stroke.

The Water for Life gallery is a little more hands-on. It shows how the water system in London has worked since Roman times, including how it was used to battle against cholera, a serious water-transmitted disease. You can walk through a cross section of the present-day Thames Water Ring Main and explore life Down Below. A kids' activity sheet makes the visit more fun.

Kids who like steam locomotives (picture Thomas the Tank Engine) should visit the two beauties in the engine shed. Even better, come on a weekend when free short rides are offered, so kids can let off some steam of their own.

HEY, KIDS! Sewers, rats, and the slightly revolting world underneath London have a magnetic appeal. Can you actually imagine the hard jobs of the people scratching around in them trying to make a living? These poor souls were called "toshers," which comes from the English slang for rubbish: tosh.

KEEP IN MIND For planning purposes, note that the trip here takes about 20 minutes by train, 30 by tube and bus; you'll most likely spend an hour or two at the museum. In addition to regular railroad weekends (when you can ride on the locomotives Cloister and Wendy), there are a host of special event weekends, including a live model-railway show, a festival of steam, and a historic fire-engine rally. The standpipe tower opens occasionally for intrepid stair climbers; on London Open House Weekend in late September, admission is free to this architecurally "listed" (landmarked) building.

LEGOLAND

Lego lovers and Duplo devotees have a ball at this theme park that combines creativity and fun. The famous building bricks become larger than life in beautiful creations, and kids can build to their heart's content or enjoy more than 50 rides geared to a range of ages. The hardest decision is how to fit everything in, so study the map and the attractions of the play zones as the Hill Train descends into the heart of the park. A good plan is to take turns waiting in line, so that everyone can enjoy the surrounding Lego constructions, which are everywhere. Some are a little harder to spot—they're hiding between the pretty plants and shrubs, and beside little waterways and bridges.

The top hot-shot rides are in the farthest points of the park, and getting wet is part of the fun. You can whiz through the water on stand-up-style jet skis in Wave Surfer, by My Town Harbour; take a quiet boat ride (with a surprise ending) in Pirate Falls in the Wild Wood; and survive a downhill dinghy chute in the X Challenge at Explore Land. Dry rides include

HEY, KIDS!
Can you guess how many bricks it takes to build the models here? More than you've got at home, for sure. The Dinosaur Family took a quarter million bricks, but maybe you could make a mini version of Little Egg, the smallest member of the family.

KEEP IN MIND Travel time from central London is about an hour. Summer, particularly during school vacation, is the busiest time here, so if you visit then, come early to avoid lines for the top rides. Summer is also the time when the most attractions are open. Check for special events, such as fireworks evenings, stunt shows, and other performances. As you'd expect, the shop sells Lego in vast quantities (including clothes). Any sets you ever wanted, plus the latest designs, can be found here.

Windsor Park, Berkshire. Rail: Windsor, then Legoland shuttle bus. Bus: Green Line bus from Victoria Station

£22.95 ages 16 and up, £19.95 children 4–15

Mar–late July and early Sept–Jan, daily 10–6 (sunset, if earlier); late July–early Sept, daily 10–8

0870/504–0404; www.lego.com

All ages

Castleland, with a soaring coaster around the fierce Dragon; the low-scream beginners' version is Dragon's Apprentice. You can find rides on a gentler scale in Traffic Zone with Boating School and L Drivers, which let you navigate along routes. For high rides with cool park views, choose from Sky Rider, Space Tower, Balloon School, Whirly Birds, Ferris Wheel, and others.

Miniland is for strolling through and admiring famous European sights re-created in Lego bricks. In London, Big Ben chimes and Tower Bridge opens to let boats through; in Paris, dancers do the cancan outside the Moulin Rouge; and in Scotland, the Loch Ness Monster lurks beneath the water. The list of instant entertainment options at Legoland is long, even without the Imagination Centre, where you can pick up tips from the pro model makers and then return home with your own building ideas.

EATS FOR KIDS There's something here to suit all tastes, including a Picnic Grove if you've brought your own treats. In Lego style, **Pizza Pergola** and **Pasta Patch** let you construct your favorite flavor combination. For fresh grilled burgers, head to the **Crossed Ribs,** near Pirate Falls. At **The Big Restaurant** you are surrounded by a seascape with fish and coral reefs, plus Lego play tables; choose anything from salads to grilled main courses.

LONDON AQUARIUM

Across the water from Big Ben, deep beneath County Hall, lurks a microcosm of underwater life. Here glass tanks containing an amazing variety of fish and other water creatures line the dappled, curving corridors. Displays of sea and river settings are divided into sections representing the waters of the world. Spend too long in the early sections, and your eyes will bulge out—just like the eyes of some fish. A good exploration takes about two hours, allowing time to hear a talk by a marine expert, feel around in the tide pools, and linger in areas that you'd otherwise have to rush through, such as the mangrove swamps toward the end.

Your journey begins with the birdsong, grass reeds, and creatures that are typical of the freshwaters of Britain and Europe. Adults may want to stay in this gentle re-creation a little longer than kids, who, after being momentarily fascinated by the luminous moon jellyfish, switch their attention to the Pacific's sharks. Swishing around between schools of smaller fish fry (the jacks), the sharks bare their fiendish, flesh-tearing teeth and flash a perpetually

EATS FOR KIDS The aquarium has no restaurant, but you can eat a picnic in a seating area with drink machines. Nearby Waterloo Station has many sandwich stands for a quick bite, and there's a **McDonald's** next door to the aquarium in County Hall, on the riverside promenade. For fishy dishes with chips (french fries), dive into the reasonably priced cab driver's haunt **Super Fish** (191 Waterloo Rd., tel. 020/7928–6924). Also see BFI London IMAX Cinema and HMS *Belfast*.

County Hall, Westminster Bridge Rd., SE1.
Tube: Waterloo, Westminster

 £8.75 ages 15 and up, £5.25
children 3–14, £25 family
ticket

Daily 10–6; last admission 5

020/7967–8000; www.
londonaquarium.co.uk

 3 and up

hungry look from their beady eyes. Circle the super-size cylindrical tank again and again as you walk down three floors to where the wonderful rays hunker down beneath the sand. At each level you can sit and stare through the glass; even tiny tots get a great look. At intervals, TV monitors show fishy documentaries, and interactive audiovisual displays let kids press buttons to find out how, for instance, the smallest fish survive.

Another don't-miss section is Seashore and Beach, where you can stroke a ray and watch such tide-pool creatures as crabs and anemones. If kids can drag themselves away from hand-dipping, they can check out the moving, darting rainbow of color of the Coral Reef, with gorgeously painted clown fish, the impressive lionfish with its venomous spines, delicate sea horses, and teeny spotted garden eels popping up from the sand. Entertaining tricks they don't do, but these guys will have you hooked for hours nonetheless.

HEY, KIDS! Ever wonder if sharks sleep? The answer is very few do and rarely, since they must swim to keep water moving over their gills. However, the nurse shark does nap on the seabed. Want something else to chew on? A sand tiger shark can go through 20,000 teeth in a lifetime. Bet that bankrupts the tooth fairy!

KEEP IN MIND As you enter, note the feeding and aquatic talk times. Generally, shark and rain-forest talks are held daily; sharks are fed Tuesday, Thursday, and Saturday at 2:30; and piranhas chow down on Monday, Wednesday, Friday, and Saturday at 1. Kids' activity sheets cost 15p–30p, and a souvenir guide has fascinating facts. County Hall is beside the British Airways London Eye (see #62) on the bank of the Thames, a good place for a fun walk after you've explored the dark depths of the watery world.

LONDON BUTTERFLY HOUSE

A tiny piece of rain forest survives at the parking lot of Syon Park in west London, on the riverbank opposite the Royal Botanic Gardens (*see #21*) at Kew. It's a butterfly house—an exotic little oasis (mainly under glass roofs and with controlled humidity) where around 1,000 little beauties and some interesting creepy crawlies live among tropical plants that grow in a garden beside a gentle cascade and pool.

The delicate little beasts are everywhere: fluttering around your head, on the plants, and even on the paths, so step carefully. Feast your eyes on *Delias eucharis, Attacus atlas,* and *Danaus plexippus*—some of the brightest of the more than 75 tropical species here. You can pick out your favorites from the signs by the door. Some butterflies are attracted by the color or scent of your clothes, so you may find them alighting on your back and shoulders. While you stroll and admire the butterflies, they are busy feeding, mating, and dying (the odd corpse does lie around), all part of their life span of about two to four weeks. You can read about this cycle by the small netted boxes, where the pupae hang on little lines.

HEY, KIDS!

Butterfly or moth? To tell the difference, look at the antennae. Butterflies have long, clublike antennae, whereas moths' antennae are furry and featherlike. For a beautiful example, watch for the giant atlas moth and compare it to the darting orange-and-black monarch butterfly.

KEEP IN MIND Just a few steps away from the butterfly house is another interesting animal attraction: Aquatic Experience (*see #68*). Another option, and one that's a welcome break after the butterfly house's humid conditions, is Syon Park (*see #13*). This sumptuous acreage contains the gardens of Syon House, home to the duke of Northumberland. (There are separate admission charges for both attractions.) If you want to cram in everything, allow at least an hour for the butterflies, another for the aquatic animals, and as long as you can for the park—it's a beauty.

Syon Park, London Rd., Brentford.
Rail: Syon La.

 £4.95 ages 17 and up,
£3.95 children 3–16, £15
family ticket

 Late Mar–mid-Oct, daily 10–5;
mid-Oct–late Mar, daily 10–3:30

020/8560–7272;
www.butterflies.org.uk

3 and up

Besides the butterflies, check out the mesmerizing, captive leaf cutter ants. Watch them scurrying along their thick rope trail, busy with their consumption of leaves—courtesy of Syon Park's trees. There's also a netted, semi-outdoor building with a cooler climate for indigenous butterflies. Look for the purple emperor, which thrives on deer droppings. Sharpen your eyesight to spot butterflies hiding underneath foliage or on the walls, as these varieties are more timid than their tropical cousins. Some birds live here, too, including soft-billed tropical species.

The final section returns to arthropods and a humid environment, with a small selection of dangerous insects such as tarantulas and scorpions. You can also see stick insects (or can you?), those wizards of camouflage. Don't miss the leopard geckos in the insect exhibit. Yes, they're lizards, but they're a lot cuter than the bugs and are a welcome addition.

EATS FOR KIDS The sweeping driveway into Syon Park is quite a hike, so you'll want to stay on the grounds to eat. Luckily, there are enough options here to satisfy. The self-service **Patio Café,** at the park entrance, serves pastas, sausages, chicken, snacks, and drinks. On the other side of the parking lot, the **Syon Park Farm Shop** sells enough delicious organic produce and snacks to let you make your own gourmet picnic.

LONDON DUNGEON

Blood, bones, and gore galore—what could be more appealing? The London Dungeon is the ultimate chamber of horrors, chronicling chilling periods in British history. You might think that children will find it too nightmarish—and some small ones do—yet strangely enough there are hordes of children eager to be scared out of their wits, making for long lines to get in, particularly on weekends and during the holiday season. Call or check the Web site for hours; they change with Easter and school vacations.

The opening exhibit gives a taste of what's to come. Scarily lifelike wax models show how grim it could be to live in medieval times (around the 14th century). You'll find out what would happen if you stole a piece of bread to feed your starving kids (you could be hanged) or spoke against the king (you could lose your tongue with the help of one of the torture instruments displayed here). If you didn't rot in prison with the rats, you might catch the plague, a pretty revolting fate, as demonstrated by a poor victim showing signs of the dreadful disease.

EATS FOR KIDS Drinks and the usual burger and fries fare are available from the on-site **restaurant**. Opposite, among the shops of the glass-roofed space called Hays Galleria, **Café Rouge** (tel. 020/7378–0097) is a brasserie serving a range of club sandwiches, salads, and upscale chicken and burger dishes. Even cheaper is the historic **George Inn** (77 Borough High St., tel. 020/7407–2056), a five-minute walk away. Owned by the National Trust, it serves more traditional British fare.

28–34 Tooley St., SE1.
Tube: London Bridge

 £14.50 ages 15 and up,
£8.25 children 5–14; check
Web for off-peak prices

 Mid-Apr–mid-July and Sept–Oct, daily
10–5:30; mid-July–Aug, daily 10–7:30;
Nov–mid-Apr, daily 10:30–5

020/7403-7221;
www.thedungeons.com

 9 and up

But this is only the mild beginning of your tour, on which costumed actor-guides take you from one historical drama to another without warning. In Judgement Day, the first "ride," you may feel like an innocent bystander, but whether or not you're guilty of any crimes, somehow you know you won't escape courtroom punishment. Further journeys into the past are linked by dark, catacomb-like passages lined with gruesome exhibits. In Jack the Ripper's London, for example, you'll witness tales of his terrible murders, after which he left his victims' insides out. In the final ride, try to survive the Great Fire of London in 1666 by running the gauntlet of flames—well, not actually, but the pyrotechnics are pretty convincing. If you do survive, you can take home a gory souvenir from the gift shop. Care for a severed arm, anyone?

The dungeon is billed as an orgy of grisly entertainment. Any child who relishes a churning stomach will think it's the best game in town.

KEEP IN MIND
You can buy tickets in advance on the Web site. Note that some exhibits, rides, and other parts of the tour are not advisable for people with weak hearts or nervous dispositions, pregnant women, or young children. Unaccompanied children under 15 are not admitted.

HEY, KIDS! London, like the rest of England and Europe, suffered from the Black Death, or bubonic plague, intermittently over 300 years. The first outbreak occurred in 1348. In 1665, the year of another major outbreak, Samuel Pepys recorded in his diary that 6,000 Londoners died in just one month. The disease, spread by flea-ridden rats, started with a rash, then fever, and swellings that turned black. Death would usually follow in two days.

LONDON'S TRANSPORT MUSEUM

The best way to get around London hassle-free is by Underground—a.k.a. the tube. But have you ever wondered how it was built, particularly the parts that run under the Thames? Here's the place to find out. The story of London transportation is told with costumed actors, from the first tunnel in the 1860s (for steam engines on the Metropolitan Line from Paddington) to the 1990s' Canary Wharf station, designed by Norman Foster. The museum occupies one of the original tall steel-and-glass-ceiling Covent Garden flower market buildings, which gives it the air of an old Victorian station.

Make your way around the museum's numbered Kidzones. There's lots to pull, turn, spin, and feel while you uncover theories of horsepower or the best way to design a bus. Most age groups will find something absorbing: tots can jump on imaginary rides on the vehicles and take the wheel of the Funbus. Young school-age kids (with parents) might try a self-guided trail with an activity sheet that encourages them to gather information before they set off to the next zone; kids collect stamps en route. The Learning Centre, good

KEEP IN MIND Train devotees can plan a visit to the Museum Depot at Acton (118–120 Gunnersbury La., W3), where there's more space for rolling stock and train paraphernalia. Guided tours (required) take place only on certain weekends, so phone ahead or check the Web site.

EATS FOR KIDS The museum has a **Caffé Nero** (a British chain), with good coffee, sandwiches, toasted panini, and cakes, and there's a space to eat any goodies you buy from the numerous cafés and delis around the piazza and in surrounding streets. For a cheap vegetarian lunch, the stalwart **Food for Thought** (31 Neal St., tel. 020/7836–0239) is a short walk away, north of the tube. A bright and buzzy basement with squashed-together tables, it offers various daily specials, all on the healthful side. Also see Covent Garden and the Theatre Museum.

Covent Garden Piazza, WC2.
Tube: Covent Garden

 020/7379-6344, 020/7565-7299
recorded info; www.ltmuseum.co.uk

 £5.95 ages 16
and up, children 15
and under free

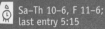 Sa–Th 10–6, F 11–6;
last entry 5:15

4 and up

for older kids, has computers for accessing the museum archives, and you can print some gorgeous vintage posters. Temporary exhibitions are accompanied by special gallery trails.

In addition, look for the costumed actor-guides, who love to talk about their jobs, from the firemen on steam trains to wartime bus conductors. There are also audiovisual sections to explore. In the oral history archive you can listen to true-life experiences of people who kept the capital moving during World War II, which was pretty harrowing. In the film archive, wonderful black-and-white footage shows how the Metropolitan Railway took shape from 1905. You can also get a taste of what it looks like to drive a tube train down a curvy, dark tunnel—not a job for the timid.

The last stop is usually the gift shop, full of sensibly priced souvenirs like an old tram car, a little red double-decker bus, and the well-known poster of the Underground map.

HEY, KIDS! If you were a young kid hanging around town in the 1880s, you could have earned a penny or two by sweeping horse dung off the streets. In those days, the most streamlined city transportation was the horse tram, and London's horse-drawn trams produced 1,000 tons of dung a day—a nice little moneymaker for eager kids!

LONDON WETLAND CENTRE

You don't need rubber boots to encounter curlews and plovers, goldeneyes and widgeons—some of the fascinating waterfowl at a unique 105-acre site about a half hour from the heart of the capital. The Wildlife and Wetland Trust has creatively transformed concrete reservoirs into a haven for freshwater-loving plants and creatures from around the world.

Your visit begins in the center's theater, where a film demonstrates that although wetlands are diminishing, they hold the key to earth's survival. This theme is expanded upon in the Discovery Centre, with its models and games full of fascinating facts. Highlighting the whole experience is the spectacular observatory, designed as a "bird airport" viewing lounge. Using the powerful telescope here, you can zoom in on new arrivals—many fowl are migratory visitors—or just watch the waterfowl diving or digging for food, or leisurely sunning their feathers. For less tranquil thrills, kids can try the video game that focuses on Terry Teal's adventurous migration voyage.

KEEP IN MIND Even if your trip turns into "nice weather for ducks" (a quaint English phrase for a rainy day), there's plenty to do during a shower. The Discovery Centre has games galore with a learning angle. Here's where, for instance, kids can try on different animal heads and find out what it's really like to get a bird's-eye (or fish's-eye) view of the world. The Pond Zone is under cover, as is the massive observatory, and you can also make a dash along the paths and watch the ducks enjoying the weather from one of the "hides," or blinds.

Queen Elizabeth's Walk, Barnes, SW13.
Tube: Hammersmith, then free Duck Bus.
Rail: Barnes, then Bus 33 or 72

 £6.75 ages 17 and up,
£4 children 4–16

 Late Mar–late Oct, daily 9:30–6;
late Oct–late Mar, daily 9:30–5; last
admission 1 hr before closing

020/8409-4400;
www.wwt.org.uk

 4 and up

Pathways radiate from the observatory and Discovery Centre to a series of global zones that leap from the Tropics to the Arctic via chirrups, quacks, and squawks from geese and ducks of many gorgeous colors. Helpful storyboards along the way make it easier to identify different species and learn more about them. Continuing on, you can walk on the Wild Side with its meandering pools and dense beds of reeds. Here, dragonflies dance above you and shy amphibians lie quietly on the ground—except for the lusty marsh frog, whose impressive croak can be heard up to 650 feet away. Serious observers will head for the Peacock Tower, with its views over the main lake and the Sheltered Lagoon; young visitors will enjoy the Pond Zone, watching minibeasts under magnifying glasses, using a net to dip into the water for creatures, or making feathered friends with tame ducks. The center is a place for young and old, at any time, as each season has its own treasures—and the conservation values learned are beyond price.

HEY, KIDS! Although as much as 70% of our planet consists of water, barely 3% is freshwater. The wetlands are places where land and water meet, such as ponds, lakes, rivers, and swamps. Just about every plant and animal group needs a place of refuge in them.

EATS FOR KIDS Shell and pebble decorations and water-themed food add whimsy to the **Water's Edge Café.** There are hot and cold buffet dishes, such as *goujons* (deep-fried strips of fish), that are good for kids. Seating is outside on the deck by the lake. If you arrive by the Hammersmith tube, you could go to **Marks & Spencer Simply Food** (27 King St., tel. 020/8741–8311), on the nearby main shopping street, for sandwiches. On the main approach road to the center, **Tesco Express** (159–167 Castlenau, no telephone), near the gas station, stocks a more limited selection of picnic fare.

LONDON ZOO

No longer places to merely stand and stare, forward-thinking zoos now spread the latest buzz on conservation and nature education, and the London Zoo is no exception. Activities go far beyond watching and meeting some of the zoo's 12,000 animals, and it's unlikely you'll cover everything in one visit. Plan to come early and allow yourself several hours.

Naturally, the big beasts are a must-see. Sometimes you need patience to get a good look, however, since some of the larger enclosures have obscuring foliage and private areas to let the endangered species take part in the captive breeding programs. The family of the magnificent Sumatran tiger Raika is one of these success stories. At the rejuvenated Bear Mountain, rare sloth bears live alongside lively langurs; you can find out how harmoniously they coexist at the afternoon bear talk. Of the traditional enclosures, the graceful 1936 Penguin Pool is a magnet for kids at penguin feeding time. The bulky gray blocks of the Casson Pavilion are where you'll find the camels (the elephants lived here until they

HEY, KIDS!

They may be the planet's smallest inhabitants, but in population, invertebrates dwarf humans. Next time you swat a fly, just think: if a pair of houseflies and a year's worth of descendants survived, they could form a ball 93 million miles across—the distance from Earth to the sun.

EATS FOR KIDS

To save the effort of carrying around extra stuff, take advantage of the on-site facilities. Bear in mind that whatever you buy (including the offerings at the well-stocked gift shop) supports the zoo's worldwide conservation work. The **Oasis Café** serves good-size portions of hot and cold meals as well as snacks. The **Picnic Shop,** a cheaper option, sells self-serve, packaged snacks to eat at the outdoor tables, and there are many grassy areas in which to sit and enjoy ices from kiosks around the zoo.

Regent's Park (Outer Circle), NW1.
Tube: Camden Town, then Bus 274

 £12 ages 15 and up,
£9 children 3–14

 Mar–Oct, daily 10–5:30; Nov–Feb,
daily 10–4; last admission 1 hour
before closing

 020/7722–3333;
www.londonzoo.co.uk

2 and up

moved to bigger spaces at the zoo's wildlife park, Whipsnade). The Reptile House is a must for Harry Potter fans, as that's where young Harry first spoke "Parseltongue." If you want to see new attractions, check out the meerkats perching on rocky outcrops; playful otters chasing around pools and waterfalls; and marmosets in a rain-forest setting.

The Amphitheatre hosts encounter sessions that could include lemurs or parrots, and at the Children's Zoo, the petting of rabbits, sheep, goats, and alpacas is encouraged. But to meet the most important beasts on the planet, you must visit BUGS! In this huge glass pavilion, you'll discover—hands-on style—the importance of biodiversity, the delicate balance between humans, animals, and insects. Kids can see plenty of minibeasts close up, such as giant millipedes and hissing cockroaches, and question the keepers. If you have time, visit the breeding section upstairs, which has a good selection of tropical partula snails. Otherwise, kids can get creative in the art workshop and play area.

KEEP IN MIND Consider these two ways to plan your day. You can follow the green footprint trail, which follows a circular route past the major exhibits; the trail can take all day in and of itself. Or you can shuttle between feeding times and animal-encounter sessions, noted on the Daily Events Sheet (available at the entrance). You may want to strike a balance between the two, as time and fatigue dictate.

MADAME TUSSAUD'S & LONDON PLANETARIUM

The collection of waxwork models of the famous (and infamous) hardly needs an introduction, but the life of Madame herself is less well known. The young Tussaud learned her skills from a doctor, who introduced her to French high society. During the French Revolution, young Marie was captured but managed to keep her head, along with her collection of death masks of guillotined nobles. She fled to England, where these gruesome models became a touring exhibition; it has been installed here since 1884. The Planetarium opened in 1958, but its activities and screen show are the latest in technology.

Your set route includes some of the original revolutionary heads and reveals how models are made. Next comes the Sporting Heroes hall, including Olympians and tennis champions, followed by Hollywood Legends and Superstars as well as by historical greats such as Abe Lincoln, Nelson Mandela, and good old Will Shakespeare. The celebrity ranks have swelled in proportion to the public's appetite for the rich and famous. You can join them at an A-list party, where you can chat with J-Lo or Brad Pitt and hear the latest gossip. To make

KEEP IN MIND Come early to get the maximum value from your tickets by having the time and energy to visit both the waxworks and planetarium. Prices change according to the season, with full details on the Web site. You also pay a bit less if you arrive later in the day; you have less time to visit, however. The information number given above lets you make credit-card bookings for timed tickets, so you can avoid standing in the sometimes lengthy lines, but there is an added £2 charge.

Marylebone Rd., NW1.
Tube: Baker St.

From £14.99 ages 16 and up,
£10.49 children 5–15

M–F 10–5:30, Sa–Su 9:30–5.30
(last admission)

0870/400–3000;
www.madame-tussauds.com

7 and up

it "virtually" more confusing, the models are talking to real people in the scene, and "paparazzi" are trying to snap the action.

It's all a fun precursor to the big thrill, however. In Chamber Live, tortured victims and notorious killers populate a world of scary sounds, scenery, and smells, with live actors to whoop it all up. (There's an extra £2 charge for this—a suitable excuse to miss this exhibit if you have younger kids in tow.)

Do you have stamina left for an intergalactic tour at the planetarium? It's well worth it, as these stars provide more than entertainment. The atmospheric Planet Zone has walls with multicolor, textured images and models of planets, and you can try games and push buttons in fact-finding missions. The high-tech show is guaranteed to thrill as your seat seemingly transmutes onto a rocket and you zoom into space.

HEY, KIDS! The real human hair used on the models requires grooming, but it isn't supposed to need a cut. Staff discovered that Adolf Hitler's appeared to be growing! Hitler doesn't get many hugs, but *Ab Fab*'s Joanna Lumley does; her jacket is often at the cleaners.

EATS FOR KIDS Madame Tussaud's has two **Costa Coffee** café areas. If your kids still have an appetite, the popular chain **Pizza Express** (Baker St. and Marylebone Rd., tel. 020/7486–0888) is consistently good, with friendly staff in bright, Italian-style surroundings, although the pizzas aren't the biggest. For a picnic in Regent's Park, nearby **M&S Simply Food** (tel. 020/7724–7467) in Marylebone Station keeps long hours.

MILLENNIUM BRIDGE

33

Not just any bridge, this more than 1,200-foot-long aluminum-and-steel span is the first new footbridge in central London in more than a century. (The Romans built the first bridge across the Thames, and the last was Tower Bridge in 1894. While traffic buzzes across Blackfriars to the west and London Bridge to the east, you can discover the joys of strolling across the river without cars thundering along beside, and stop to admire the beautiful views. Designed by Norman Foster—the architect of many eye-catching buildings on the London skyline and worldwide—and sculptor Anthony Caro, the bridge connects the old (elegant, domed St. Paul's Cathedral) and the new (stark, red, oversize Tate Modern art museum) and stands smack in the middle of the Millennium Mile, a riverside walkway that takes in a clutch of popular sights on the South Bank.

The bridge opened in a blaze of publicity on a breezy weekend in June 2000, and people lined up by the thousands to enjoy the so-called "blaze of light" streaking across the

EATS FOR KIDS Buy gourmet sandwiches from **Sarnis** (Gabriel's Wharf, tel. 020/7928–6654) and picnic in Bernie Spain Gardens, by the OXO Tower. Or choose from 40 types of pancakes at **House of Crêpes** (Gabriel's Wharf, tel. 020/7401–9816), also on the South Bank. See St. Paul's Cathedral and Tate Modern.

KEEP IN MIND After walking the bridge, why not walk the Millennium Mile on the South Bank? Actually, this much-visited section of the river contains two other walks: the Thames Path and the Jubilee Walk (with 1977 Silver Jubilee markers). Free maps are available at the St. Paul's Churchyard Information Centre. If you are interested in the area's history, discover more about the river and its bridges in an excellent display at the Museum in Docklands (see #30). Those who like footbridges can explore the Hungerford Bridge, which opened in 2003 and flanks the Charing Cross railroad bridge.

Bankside, SE1. Tube: Southwark (south),
St. Paul's (north)

Bridge daily 24 hrs. Information Centre
Apr–Sept, daily 9:30–5; Oct–Mar, M–F
9:30–5, Sa 9:30–12:30

Free

020/7332–1456 Information
Centre, St. Paul's Churchyard.
www.cityoflondon.gov.uk

All ages

Thames. The graceful, gleaming bridge does appear to fly effortlessly over the water, but its very lightness, plus the overwhelming hordes on that first weekend, caused some swaying. Visitors had their moving experience all right. Even though some swinging is expected with suspension bridges, the engineers were unsettled enough to close it. The bridge's re-opening coincided with the Queen's Golden Jubilee in 2002.

The views are breathtaking, none more so than that of St. Paul's looming before you— the best river view of the cathedral and an artistic photo op. You can look downriver to the Tower of London, Tower Bridge, and beyond, and up to Somerset House, with the London Eye and Big Ben rising above the river bend. Down below, boats bustle back and forth. Don't forget to give a wave to people on the sightseeing boats, who don't have the same chance you do to stop and enjoy.

HEY, KIDS! Christopher Wren, the architect of St. Paul's, might have given up if he'd had the same problems the builders of this bridge had. Work that was already behind schedule came to a sudden halt so that a rare breed of snail found on some old jetty legs could be rehoused, to the tune of more than £50,000. It just goes to show that small creatures can wield big power.

MONUMENT

32

The simply named monument designed by Christopher Wren to commemorate the Great Fire of London and its victims in 1666 was the tallest single column in the world when it was completed in 1677. Scaling its 311 steps is not for the fainthearted or weary, and is guaranteed to tire even the most hyper kid. At 202 feet, the summit is the same distance from the base as the site where the fire began, at a bakery in Pudding Lane. A trip to the top rewards climbers with a wonderful view of Wren's graceful churches and the latest high-rise buildings. You also receive a special certificate to prove that you made the climb.

The story of the Great Fire is a cruel one. It raged for days, turning the city into an inferno. When the fire finally burned itself out, 87 churches and 13,200 houses had been lost, and all that remained were the smoking ruins of the medieval walled city. The only blessings were that it solved London's overcrowding problem in one blow and that only nine lives were lost. The king's baker, Mr. Farryner, swore that he had raked the oven's embers that

KEEP IN MIND A joint ticket is available for the Monument and Tower Bridge Experience (*see #7*). Climbing the Monument is not recommended for those with claustrophobia or carrying babies or for small children. Indeed, it shudders with the passing of each vehicle below. The famous diarist James Boswell found the experience unnerving: ". . . so monstrous a way up in the air, so far above London and all its spires." An earlier diarist, Samuel Pepys, wrote commentary that's used in a small video reenactment illuminating the Great Fire in the Museum of London (*see #29*), which also gives the facts behind the fire.

Monument St., EC2.
Tube: Cannon St., Monument

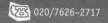
020/7626-2717

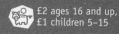
£2 ages 16 and up,
£1 children 5–15

Daily 10–6

7 and up

night. Flour is combustible, though, and there were no gaps between the bakery and adjoining houses to slow the spreading flames.

While the city's destruction is represented by a gilt bronze urn licked by flames on top of the Monument, inscriptions around the base chart King Charles II's efforts to rebuild London with the help of Christopher Wren. The view from the top confirms the latter's genius. You may locate some of Wren's most famous churches nearby, such as St. Stephen Walbrook, St. Bride's, and St. Mary-le-Bow, although his work doesn't predominate as remarkably as it did 300 years ago, when St. Paul's was the tallest building on the skyline. Now the cathedral is dwarfed by tall techno towers such as the Nat West Tower and the Lloyd's building. Back then it was a once-in-a-lifetime, jelly-leg experience to mount the steps and walk out onto the viewing platform.

HEY, KIDS! When the old St. Paul's Cathedral began to burn during the height of the fire, molten lead from its roof rained down onto the streets. Wren, the architect of the Monument, was put to work after the fire to build a bigger, greater St. Paul's, which you see today.

EATS FOR KIDS Weekdays, when the City is in full buzz, visit **Fuego** (1A Pudding La., tel. 020/7929–3366), a family-friendly Spanish restaurant aptly named after the Great Fire. The many tapas (small dishes) and larger menu choices, such as battered prawns, a steak sandwich with fries and salad, and paella, can be shared. On the weekend, when many City places are closed, cross London Bridge to the bistro-style **Café Rouge** (Hays Galleria, off Tooley St., tel. 020/7378–0097), which has more steak and fries, chicken, and steak sandwiches.

MOUNTFITCHET CASTLE

Castles and kids just go together, and this castle in the Essex countryside—40 minutes by train and an hour by car from central London—is a prime destination. It's a Norman "motte and bailey" (a walled feudal castle atop a hill), with dwellings reconstructed from ruins. To visit is to imagine life for peasants and Norman lords and ladies 900 years ago.

Don't be charmed by the folksy huts and buildings. After a look inside, you realize life was anything but charming, though the deer, hens, and goats that wander around *are* cute. (The castle shop sells food packets to feed them.) Otherwise, life was tough, as you'll learn while walking around the signposted huts, where waxwork models—blacksmith, brewer, weaver, alchemist, potter, cook, candlemaker—go about, and tell about (with voice recordings), their daily tasks.

Grim reminders of punishments meted out are apparent. In the prison you see a victim with his hand freshly chopped off—he'd probably stolen some of the castle's deer. The

KEEP IN MIND As the village and parkland are outside, plan to visit in good weather. Should the day dampen, head to the House on the Hill Toy Museum, next door (10% off admission with castle ticket). It holds a fair-size collection, from teddy bears to Victorian trains.

EATS FOR KIDS A **café** here serves a small range of food from this century, and if the weather's good, you can picnic on the pretty grounds. Stansted village has tea shops and village pubs for hot meals. If you have a car, you can drive to the nearby village of Rickling Green (heading north, just off B1383) and try the **Cricketers Arms** (Rickling Village Green, tel. 01799/543210). At this pub you can order sandwiches, steaks, and children's meals, and eat amid cozy cricketing memorabilia.

Stansted, Essex.
Rail: Stansted, Mountfitchet

 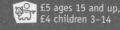 £5 ages 15 and up,
£4 children 3–14

 Mid-Mar–mid-Nov, daily 10–5

01279/813237;
www.gold.enta.net

4 and up

offender hanging from the gallows would have committed a more serious crime, and the stocks, which you can try on for size, were for petty misdemeanors. You wouldn't dare get sick, either; take a look inside the surgeon's hut, which more closely resembles a butcher's room. If you want to know more about anything you see, ask one of the costumed villagers strolling around. You may even meet the baron Richard de Montfitchet or his lady.

The castle walls kept out invaders, so to live inside them was a privilege—hard to believe when you peek in the community house where 30 people would have lived with their animals. Climb up the siege tower to look for rebels, and find out how to stop them with the dastardly looking, towering catapult, which took 15 men to operate. Defense wasn't always successful; in the peasant's hut, you learn of a ransack by the feared Vikings. It's a wild, wild world to discover, and you'll be jolly thankful you can return to the comfort of modern times.

HEY, KIDS! The grassy surroundings here are a far cry from the nasty conditions you would have seen in Norman times. Back then it would have been muddy and full of foul smells, rats, and disease. Even the baron would have to endure beggars and dogs eating scraps off the floor in the banqueting hall, thrown by the generous diners.

MUSEUM IN DOCKLANDS

The location of this museum about London's port, on a cobbled quayside beside water that reflects the gigantic modern tower of No. 1 Canada Square, brilliantly contrasts the old and the new at Canary Wharf. It's just a speedy ride from Bank station on the slick Docklands Light Railway, or you can arrive by boat; the journey is a mini-adventure in itself. Then there's the romance of the building—an early-19th-century warehouse for coffee, tea, sugar, rum, and West Indian imports—with original wood floor, beams, and pillars. Miraculously, it survived after the Luftwaffe rained down bombs in World War II. Regeneration, as the museum makes clear, is the strength of the Docklands. The port that became the warehouse for the world, stuffed with feathers, furs, and spices, has seen trade go elsewhere. Today converted warehouse lofts and new riverside housing have become some of the coolest and most adventurous choices for London living.

You start on Floor 3 and wind your way along the fascinating, 2,000-year story of the port, which is told through films, push-button links, and engaging displays. Roaming visitor

EATS FOR KIDS The museum **Coffee Stop** (and the gift shop, with a great selection of books) can be accessed via the museum or direct from the quayside. Light and airy, the café serves sandwiches and snacks inspired by the flavors of the Indies. Part of the warehouse building, the bar and lounge **1802** is more sophisticated, though it's okay for older kids. Within Canada Square at Canary Wharf are more cafés and supermarkets for picnic supplies. Cozy and local, **Booty's** (92A Narrow St., tel. 020/7987–8343) has a riverside view; children are admitted in the eating area.

No. 1 Warehouse, West India Quay,
Hertsmere Rd., E14. Tube: Canary Wharf.
DLR: West India Quay

0870/444–3855;
www.museumindocklands.org.uk

 £5 ages 17 and up,
children 16 and under free;
tickets valid for 1 year

Daily 10–6

4 and up

assistants provide further explanation and interesting anecdotes. The port of London was an exciting place, busy with trade and people coming and going. Bridges were crucial; check out the scale model of the first stone bridge in Tudor times. Walk through buildings that have been brilliantly re-created so that you can examine the scales and other port equipment, and peer into candlelit rooms and offices.

On the next floor, Sailortown is dark, dingy, and seedy, with its warren of streets, a walk-in pub, shops, and lodging rooms: it's perfect for dubious goings-on. The Docklands at War section is compelling, with a film of the blitz known as Black Saturday. Further displays chart later development, but by now younger kids will want to let off steam. Mudlarks, the children's gallery, is stuffed with learning activities. Kids can sniff and guess smells, load a clipper ship, construct Canary Wharf, and get wet delving for "antiquities." All in all, there's enough here to keep you going for the day.

KEEP IN MIND

A short section of the sign-posted Thames Path (www. nationaltrails.gov.uk) makes a fun riverside walk. To the east are Island Gardens and a fantastic vista of the Queen's House and Royal Naval College in Greenwich. A walk west takes you to Tower Bridge, past wharfs and pubs.

HEY, KIDS!

Pirates were the scourge of the Thames, so punishment for piracy was gruesome. The gibbet cage on display in the museum would suspend a specially tarred dead body within it; the tar prevented the body from disintegrating too quickly in the water. There was even a notorious female pirate, Mary Read, who also came to a grim end, dying in prison from a fever. At Wapping Old Stairs, by the romantically named Waterside Gardens, pirates were hanged, then tied to a stake at the foot of the steps, where the tide would wash over them.

MUSEUM OF LONDON

Before Buckingham Palace, before the Tower of London, fields covered the land, and hairy beasts and cave dwellers lived in what is now a modern metropolis. This engaging urban history museum shows the city's metamorphosis over many centuries. The constantly updated galleries display everything from animal bones to workmen's tobacco pipes. Touch the screens of the computers to discover more information, but chatting with a guide in period costume or handling some ancient objects is more fun, so find out about the day's scheduled events when you arrive.

You can walk through the museum chronologically, visiting a series of re-created sets such as a Roman living room and an 18th-century prison cell. The Victorian street is very Charles Dickens; the confectioner's shop has huge jars of traditional candies that were sold by the ounce. You can also get a handle on everyday tools and objects, such as unusual weighing machines, and check out the Tudor jewelry, which looks cool enough for today.

KEEP IN MIND The latest events and finds are listed at the entrance and on the museum's Web site; one of these is the discovery of Roman Londinium's "lost" amphitheater, now open at the Guildhall. The Museum in Docklands (see #30) is a branch of the museum.

EATS FOR KIDS The spacious **café** does a good job with soups, salads, and sandwiches; it's the best bet on weekends, when most eating places in the financial district shut down. Main courses also come in child portions, or try Kids Lunchboxes, with a sandwich, fruit, and a juice drink. When the weather's fine, sit outside and try the organic ice creams, cookies, and cakes. The nearby Barbican Centre's **Waterside Café** (Silk St., tel. 020/7638–4141) sells similar fare and has outdoor tables; there's space for kids to stretch their legs. On Sunday, the Barbican's **Balcony Bistro** (Silk St., tel. 020/7628–3331) serves brunch, with newspapers.

London Wall, EC2.
Tube: Barbican, St. Paul's

 Free

 M–Sa 10–5:50, Su 12–5:50

0870/444-3852 voice, 0870/444-3851
recording; www.museumoflondon.org.uk

 6 and up

Another approach is to head for the bigger galleries. The largest, World City, charts the years 1789 to 1914, including the stories of the entrepreneurs who put the "Great" into Britain and also grappled with the problem of the polluted city's Great Stink. The Medieval Gallery follows the river highway and its importance to the city's growth; this section has many fun but gruesome displays, such as skeletal remains from the Black Death. There's also a facial reconstruction of London's oldest woman, discovered on a farm in Shepperton. Don't miss Oliver Cromwell's death mask, Queen Victoria's enormous crinolined gowns, or the Great Fire diorama, with flickering flames and diary extracts from Samuel Pepys.

Epitomizing hip London are Vivienne Westwood's walk-defying, sky-high designer shoes and a colorful float from the Notting Hill Carnival. Tradition is well represented with the glitzy coach used by the Lord Mayor for his centuries-old annual parade through the City. And you can see through a window a preserved piece of the old city wall built by the Romans—hence the street name "London Wall" in the museum's address.

HEY, KIDS! As the story goes, Dick Whittington came to London to seek his fortune, but when he didn't make money, he turned tail. As he was leaving, he looked back on the city, and the church bells, along with a black cat, told him to "turn again, Whittington." He did, and he became a great mayor four times over between 1391 and 1419. Don't confuse this mayor with the newer position of mayor of London. The traditional Lord Mayor is elected annually by the ancient livery companies of the City of London (the City isn't the whole city but one of London's oldest neighborhoods).

More compact than the Imperial War Museum (*see #45*), this place tells the soldier's story from the country's first professional army—the Yeomen of the Guard—to the sophisticated British land forces of today, through paintings, photographs, uniforms, and equipment. A tour of the gallery begins with the Redcoats, from Henry V and the crucial Battle of Agincourt in France in 1415 (the Brits won) to the army of George III, which fought in the American colonies (the Brits lost). Other campaigns chronicled include Wellington versus Napoleon; don't miss the skeleton of the emperor's favorite horse and the saw used for rapid on-field amputations—ouch!

Wonderful battlefield models show the strategies employed, while life-size uniformed models are faithfully executed. Looking at them close up is interesting enough, but you can even try on some pieces, such as a heavy, uncomfortable helmet from the English Civil War (in which the Republican Roundheads fought the dashingly dressed Royalist Cavaliers to defeat the monarchy). In a display of arms and armor, you can lift a hefty cannonball

HEY, KIDS! In the 18th century, women weren't allowed in the army, but some disguised themselves as soldiers and went anyway. Some went purely for the adventure; others were trying to find husbands or boyfriends who were missing.

Royal Hospital Rd., SW3.
Tube: Sloane Sq.

 Free

Daily 10–5:30

020/7730–0717;
www.national-army-museum.ac.uk

6 and up

and then imagine its destructive effects in battle. The modern army is covered through re-creations of a World War I trench and a Burmese jungle, as well as archival footage from both world wars, a piece of the Berlin Wall, and exhibits on the Gulf War and the Balkans. An interactive computer section tests your military skills, from recognizing the uniforms and insignia of various regiments to surviving in a jungle expeditionary force. It's not all *Band of Brothers*, however, as the effects of war on civilians are presented, too.

In summer, costumed guides play historical roles, from archers in the Middle Ages to people doing vital jobs behind the front line, such as a female dispatch rider from World War II. You might meet up with one of Florence Nightingale's nurses; during the Crimean War in 1854, they pioneered the need for hygiene. In those days, more soldiers were likely to die from diseases picked up in hospitals than from wounds suffered in battle.

KEEP IN MIND
The souvenir shop here is a great place for fanatics of all things military, both national and international. You'll find model soldiers and a good range of books on military subjects.

EATS FOR KIDS The museum's **café** prepares light meals, but for a budget main dish, such as spaghetti Bolognese, for around £5, and a dessert of the day, the **Stockpot** (273 King's Rd., tel. 020/7823–3175) and its neighbor **Chelsea Kitchen** (98 King's Rd., tel. 020/7589–1330) are hard to beat.

NATIONAL GALLERY

More than 2,000 pictures by western Europe's great masters are displayed in this enormous collection, including a few of the most famous works of art in the world. The museum's dignified, pillared building is part of London's celebrated Trafalgar Square, with its fountains, lions, and Nelson's Column. Today the square, known as "London's living room," is totally pedestrian-friendly and tranquil.

With such a vast wealth at your disposal, where should you start? You could begin with the Renaissance and go see the real Madonna (not the singer), *The Virgin of the Rocks*, by Leonardo da Vinci, hung in the modern Sainsbury Wing. The West Wing has Titian and Hans Holbein, the artist who made it big by painting such kings as Henry VIII. Then skip a century or two to the North Wing, for portraits and more by Dutch masters like Jan Vermeer and Rembrandt, and move on to the East Wing for the Venice of Canaletto, the very British landscapes of John Constable, sea battles and sunsets by J. M. W. Turner, the France of Claude Monet, and works by Post-Impressionists Vincent van Gogh and Paul Cézanne.

HEY, KIDS!
Did you know that crushed-up insects make the beautiful red paint called carmine? Old masters used the red pigment from dead female kermes beetles, and a similar dye, known as cochineal (from the insect of the same name), was also used.

KEEP IN MIND Have a pencil ready for filling out the tour booklets. Otherwise, you'll have to choose one from one of the gallery's shops, which also carry beautiful posters, drawing pads, and postcards. The shop at the Orange Street entrance (open weekdays) specializes in kids' educational activities. Outside, the redesign of Trafalgar Square has made the gallery truly a part of the square. Many outdoor activities link the two; for full details, see the gallery information desk.

Trafalgar Sq., WC2. Tube: Charing Cross

 Free

 W 10–9, Th–T 10–6

020/7747–2885;
www.nationalgallery.org.uk

4 and up

Fine-tune your visit online in the Micro Gallery, where you can print out information along with a personally planned tour—great for older kids.

Another option is to join one of the free one-hour tours that depart daily at 1:30 and 2:30 or a tailored family session at 11:30 on weekends that includes a drop-in drawing and activity session for budding Leonardos. The information desk has details. Self-guiding themed tour booklets, good for children 4–11, direct you to different parts of the gallery and invite kids to look, think, draw, or write poems. The booklets help kids explore great works from a livelier angle, and parents aiding kids may end up seeing more than they expected to, as well. If your kids are older, you may be able to study the rest of a gallery in comparative peace while your kids are occupied with the booklet—then everyone's a cultural winner.

EATS FOR KIDS The self-service **café**, in the basement of the main building, is open daily, offering sandwiches, snacks, and drinks. The up-scale **Crivelli's Garden** (020/7747–2869), in the Sainsbury Wing, has an Italian menu, as well as a great view over Trafalgar Square. **Texas Embassy Cantina** (Cockspur St., tel. 020/7925–0077), on a triangular western part of Trafalgar Square, serves standard Tex-Mex fare.

NATIONAL MARITIME MUSEUM

As citizens of an island nation, Britons have a deep respect for the sea, and the world's largest maritime museum is the ideal place to get the full story. The building and its location—in rolling parkland by the Thames, with panoramic views of London—are picture-perfect, and arriving by boat from Westminster or Tower Pier is part of the total H_2O experience.

A visit to this brilliantly modernized museum can be rather like embarking on boats of all shapes and sizes from over the centuries, even as you keep an eye on the power of the sea. Humans inhabit just a small part of the planet, while the oceans are vast; potent reminders of this are the flashing lighthouse light and massive revolving propeller from a navy frigate that dominate the entrance. From a central, glass-covered courtyard with "streets" that highlight the past (in the shape of *Implacable*, from the Battle of Trafalgar), present (shipbuilding and containers), and future (balancing trade and ecology), you can launch off to wherever your interest takes you. Computers dot the galleries and supply facts in greater depth.

KEEP IN MIND Allow at least a day to discover all the treasures in Greenwich. Assuming you have enough energy to explore further, the Royal Observatory (*see #18*) and Queen's House (also free admission) are part of the National Maritime Museum buildings. The observatory is a short walk through the park, where you'll want to let kids run around and stand astride the famous meridian line of longitude.

Romney Rd., Greenwich, SE10.
Tube: Cutty Sark

020/8858–4422 voice, 020/8312–6565
recording; www.nmm.ac.uk

 Free

Daily 10–5

7 and up

If seafaring adventures are your thing, you can overdose in the Explorers gallery. From the swashbuckling Francis Drake to Captain James Cook, who searched for passages to link the seas across the world, to the courageous Antarctic explorer Robert F. Scott, history is covered comprehensively. The story of the *Titanic* wreck provides a backdrop for examining today's high-tech underwater exploration. If you prefer cruising to adventure, try a vintage, luxurious ocean-liner cabin in Passengers, but spare a thought for the immigrants crowded in steerage below. Don't miss the Nelson gallery, complete with all the battle facts as well as the admiral's damaged uniform.

In Nelson's day and earlier, children were part of a hard-working crew, and in The Bridge and All Hands galleries kids can try their skill at steering a Viking ship (hint: terribly difficult), loading a cargo vessel, and firing a cannon. They'll learn a little while they have loads of fun.

EATS FOR KIDS
The nautically styled **restaurant** has a terrace and views of Greenwich Park. The changing menu lists meat, fish, and vegetarian options, and kids' portions are generally available on request. A special kids' picnic area in the museum is outfitted submarine style.

HEY, KIDS! Maritime doesn't just mean having to do with boats and navigation; it means having to do with the sea. The ocean is one of the world's great resources: 97% of the planet's water is stored in the oceans, of which we use around 1%. On your way out of the museum, look at the Sphere in the glass-covered courtyard and think a little about humanity's role in preserving the fragile balance of life.

NATIONAL PORTRAIT GALLERY

The world's largest collection of portraits, both painted and photographic, is presented in a cool setting that's worth a visit even though the museum is dwarfed in size by its neighbor, the National Gallery (*see #27*). A glass-encased escalator gives you a great bird's-eye view as you travel upward on a chronological ride in reverse, from modern times up—er, back—to the 1400s and the Tudor Galleries, a good place to begin. In those times, portraiture was the equivalent of political propaganda. Take Henry VIII: in Holbein's portrait the powerful king is made to look larger than life. Elizabeth I is immortalized with her white face and jewels.

Even though some early old master portraits appear a little dark and dingy to kids, the gallery helps present them in a new light through crafty activities. A kit, available from the information desk, has plenty of ideas for things kids 7 and up can do. They can copy portraits with fuzzy felt, match fabric swatches with designs they spot in the paintings, or make flamboyant mustaches like those on some gentlemen in Victorian Gallery portraits.

KEEP IN MIND It's a good idea to call ahead for details about special free children's and family activities (tel. 020/7312–2483) or check at the information desk as you enter.

EATS FOR KIDS The **Portrait Restaurant** (tel. 020/7312–2490) is run by a top London chef, and the ambience, view, and food are outstanding. Down a level or two, in the basement next to the excellent bookshop, the **Portrait Café** is a more convenient stop for soups and sandwiches. Just opposite the gallery, **Café in the Crypt** (St. Martin-in-the-Fields, tel. 020/7839–4342) offers a hot budget lunch or salad bar, and you can tie that in with a free lunchtime chamber concert in the church (Tuesday and Thursday at 1:05), to soothe your soul as well your body. Also see the National Gallery.

St. Martin's Pl., WC2.
Tube: Charing Cross, Leicester Sq.

 Free

 Sa–W 10–6, Th–F 10–9

 020/7306–0055 voice, 020/7312–2463
recording; www.npg.org.uk

7 and up

The Weldon Gallery showcases a wealth of talented characters from the Regency period. Among the great names in frames are Mary Shelley, with scientist Humphry Davy who inspired her novel, *Frankenstein*; Admiral Nelson, with his love, Lady Hamilton; Jane Austen, painted by her sister Cassandra; and monumental writers Lord Byron, William Wordsworth, John Keats, Walter Scott, and Samuel Coleridge. It's a brainy tour de force, but if period style isn't to your family's taste, zoom back down to famous faces from the 1950s to the 1990s, including Princess Diana, Winston Churchill, Liz Taylor, and Paul McCartney, and artists like David Hockney and Andy Warhol, sometimes more famous than their subjects.

If trad portraits don't appeal, focus on the changing photographic displays such as Patrick Lichfield's gorgeous, glossy fashion mag pics, and contemporary retrospectives such as caricaturist Gerald Scarfe's take on politicians and pop stars. It's all free.

HEY, KIDS! Look for the portrait of Nell Gwyn in the 17th- and 18th-century gallery on the second floor. A beautiful actress who started her career as an orange seller, she became more famous for her role as the long-time mistress of Charles II than for her acting at the nearby Theatre Royal, on Drury Lane. The original version of this famous old London theater dated from 1663, but it burned down twice. Today's incarnation, completed in 1812, contains a huge auditorium that stages blockbuster musicals.

Huge Gothic-style arches and spires with sculpted animals merely hint at the wonders to be discovered inside this treasure house. As you enter, a diplodocus skeleton—so large it almost fills the entire hall—greets you. From here, choose from the corridors leading off into the museum's vast acreage. Be selective—if you try to cover it all, you may become fossilized, too.

The Life Galleries, reached by Waterhouse Way, contain the dinosaurs, most kids' favorite exhibit. A suspended walkway lets you look the stars of *Jurassic Park* practically in the eye. At its end, a lifelike diorama shows ferocious hunters in a feeding frenzy, complete with gruesome sounds (younger kids might find this too scary). Arthropods were around before dinosaurs, and they are introduced, in larger-than-life form, in Creepy-crawlies. A look around the mock kitchen and its uninvited visitors at No. 1 Crawley House is guaranteed to repulse—washcloths and garbage teeming with bugs, and you don't even want to know what's on the food. Aimed at older kids, Human Biology in Gallery 22 shows what we're made of and

KEEP IN MIND At Investigate, kids can experience what it's like to be a scientist, as they handle some of the museum's hoard of ancient bones, skin, teeth, preserved bugs, and more. Friendly helpers show you how to weigh, measure, magnify, and discover more on computer about how these treasures fit into the circle of life. There are myriad insects, for instance, not visible to the eye, to study under a microscope. In the courtyard garden you can watch living organisms and their seasonal changes.

Cromwell Rd., SW7.
Tube: South Kensington

Free

M–Sa 10–5:50, Su 11–5:50;
Investigate T–F 2:30–5, Sa 10:30–5,
Su 11:30–5

020/7942–5000;
www.nhm.ac.uk

5 and up; Investigate
7 and up

how we survive; stand in the unborn baby and womb exhibit to get a sense of what life is like before birth.

On your way to the Earth Galleries you can touch objects that mark evolution itself: massive mollusk shells, whales' teeth, and million-year-old rocks. Simulations and sets demonstrate the earth's more spectacular restless movements, such as a video taken during the earthquake at Kobe, Japan, in which a supermarket floor shakes beneath you. Older kids like the Earth Lab, where they can use fossils and precious rocks, with the aid of museum scientists, to discover secrets of the earth.

The accessible Darwin Centre presents creatures great and small (22 million of them) in their pickling jars and vats, from tiny frogs to the giant Komodo dragon lizard. The center provides a unique opportunity to see these wonders close up and to get behind the scenes of a scientific research institution.

EATS FOR KIDS
Kids with monster appetites find plenty at the **Life Galleries Restaurant,** by the dinosaur exhibit. Lunches include penne pasta, Cumberland sausage, sandwiches, cakes, and kids' lunchboxes at £3.50. By the Earth Galleries, the **Global Café** serves hot soups, filled baguettes, and cookies.

HEY, KIDS! Cheese skippers sound pretty tasty, but don't be fooled. They're not some exciting new crunchy snack in a bag, but rather what you might find if flying maggots have transformed your favorite lump of cheese into a nice, cozy nursery. And there are many other bugs to check out in Creepy-crawlies, possibly some you have in your kitchen. An Explore tour (ask at the main information desk) will tell you more about this and other exhibits.

REGENT'S CANAL

From Little Venice to Camden, a beautiful stretch of the Regent's Canal is one of London's best-kept secrets. Cutting through the leafy northern section of Regent's Park and at times almost invisible from the busy roads above, the canal is its own tranquil world. Willows trail in the gently lapping water, waterbirds buzz about their business, and stately herons stand still as statues. Magnificent houses with palatial private gardens sweep down to the water at Regent's Park, and the charming small backyards of Camden's tall houses come with their own bobbing rowboats.

The easiest way to explore is on a tour given by Jason Canal Boats, out of Little Venice. From the elegant stucco houses that overlook the canal and little basin (marina), it's easy to see how this oasis got its name. The tiny, tree-filled Browning Island, named after the poet Robert Browning, who lived within sight, is lined with gaily painted houseboats, which also appear at other basins farther along the canal. The *Jason* is similarly rigged out. Once inside, you can well imagine how compact you'd have to be to live in one.

EATS FOR KIDS
Jason's restaurant, canalside, has a set two-course lunch Monday–Thursday. Potato chips and drinks are sold on the boat. **Red Pepper** (8 Formosa St., tel. 020/7266–2708) is a jolly pizzeria. Pizzas are large, so kids can share. Near Camden Lock are restaurants and take-out places galore.

KEEP IN MIND The London Waterbus Company (tel. 020/7482–2550 voice, 020/7482–2660 recording) connects Camden Lock and Little Venice, stopping at the London Zoo (zoo admission available at waterbus office, Camden Lock). Hourly service runs daily April–October, weekends November–March. To enjoy the canal for free, walk the towpath, open dawn–dusk. The prettiest part is from Camden Lock to Prince Albert Bridge, where you can access Regent's Park. For a nontourist route, go east from Camden Lock to picturesque St. Pancras Lock, where you can take the bridge to Euston Road and St. Pancras Station, near the British Library.

Jason Boats, Blomfield Rd., W9.
Tube: Warwick Ave. Museum, 12–13
New Wharf Rd., N1. Tube: King's Cross

020/7286–3428 boats, 020/7713–0836
museum; www.jasons.co.uk,
www.canalmuseum.org.uk

Boat trips £6.95
round-trip; museum
£2.50, £1.25
children 9–18

Apr–Sept, daily 10:30, 12:30, 2:30,
plus 4:30 Sa–Su July–Aug; Oct, daily
12:30, 2:30; museum T–Su 10–4:30

All ages

A guide provides lively commentary along the 45-minute nonstop ride. One of the highlights is passing through part of the London Zoo, where you can get a bird's-eye view of the Snowdon Aviary, see an antelope or two ambling about, and catch a whiff of the giraffe house. Among the historical anecdotes, you discover that the canal was a working route, where boats laden with goods were pulled along the towpath by horses. At a tunnel, the horses were unhitched and the boatmen had to "leg" through it. The men lay on their backs on planks aboard the boat and "walked" the boat, using the tunnel sides. (If this fascinates you, leg along eastward to the London Canal Museum.)

Above the towpath at Camden Lock and journey's end, a marketplace teems with life. Craft shops and trendy fashion stalls are a mecca for teens and twentysomethings, a marked contrast to the gentle lull of life below the bridge.

HEY, KIDS! More than 100 years ago, ice used to be imported from Norway by ship and then brought by canal to be stored at the ice warehouse at King's Cross for Carlo Gatti. This famous ice-cream maker sold his treats to the rich across town. Poor kids would run after the horse-drawn delivery carts and lick what they could, more than likely passing on a few free germs to the purchasers. At the London Canal Museum you can peer down into the huge Victorian ice well and learn all about canals, as well as ices.

REGENT'S PARK

P robably the most perfect of London's parks, the 18th-century Regent's Park was designed by John Nash for the Prince Regent. The elegant terraces of grand, white-stuccoed houses sweep the Outer Circle's perimeter and buffer this haven from traffic noise. An Inner Circle connects many recreational areas, too, such as open spaces for playing (you might find a baseball game to crash), playgrounds, fragrant flower gardens, a boating lake, tennis courts, and an open-air theater.

Start from York Gate, between the Regent's Park and Baker Street tubes, where York Bridge leads to the Inner Circle and the gilded gates to Queen Mary's Gardens. Come to this stunning floral epicenter in June and breathe in the scents of the magnificent rose garden. Traipse across the Japanese bridge (if it's not blocked by a bridal party) to discover a cascade and duck island in a little lake. Look carefully, and you may see a "posing" heron. Also nearby are a waterfall and fountains with tiny pergola "secret" gardens. If you time it right, you can see a children's play at the open-air theater (open June–September). Shakespeare's *A*

EATS FOR KIDS **Park Cafés** are situated across the park: the one at Queen Mary's Gardens has the largest menu, often with seasonal choices of pasta, chicken, soup, salads, and snacks; in summer, eat alfresco surrounded by roses. The slightly smaller, chalet-style **café** on the Broad Walk also has a varied menu with delicious soups and sticky pastries. At the boating lake and playgrounds, kiosks sell sandwiches, ices, and drinks. Alternatively, check out the gourmet snacks at **Pret a Manger** (120 Baker St., tel. 020/7486–2264) if arriving via Baker Street tube. Also see Madame Tussaud's & London Planetarium.

Regent's Park, W1. Tube: Baker St.,
Camden Town, Regent's Park

020/7486–7905, 0870/060–1811 theater;
www.royalparks.gov.uk, openairtheatre.org

 Free

 Daily sunrise–sunset

All ages

Midsummer Night's Dream never had a more perfect setting, except when it rains—still, the show goes on.

Outside the Inner Circle (almost where you started) is a lake where you can rent a rowboat for an hour and navigate around a wildfowl island. Paddleboats are smaller but just as much fun. For more action, kids can bounce around in one of three playgrounds. Maps are posted at many entrances, or get one from the Information Centre, at the east end of the Inner Circle, by Chester Road.

Peer through the railings of the London Zoo (*see #35*), and see some of the animals for free. A camel, elephants, exotic birds, and an occasional roaring lion are on the left side of the zoo, the wolf wood is to the right, and giraffes are opposite the entrance. For smaller wildlife, visit the leafy canalside (*see* Regent's Canal), where barges ferry visitors from Camden Lock to Little Venice.

KEEP IN MIND Primrose Hill, to the north, on the far side of the Regent's Canal and Prince Albert Road, is part of Regent's Park. Climb up to its grassy hilltop (no more primroses, alas), and you'll be rewarded with a superb panorama of the park and the London skyline.

HEY, KIDS! As you walk across the beautifully landscaped lawns and among the formal flower beds, watch your step. During World War II, the park was used by the military, and no fewer than 300 bombs (including German V2 rockets) fell on the grounds. The once undulating land was flattened by infilling with dumped bomb rubble. Even today (though not very often, so don't worry too much), the ground can cave in where the fill is loose and where there are pockets or old air-raid shelters.

ROYAL BOTANIC GARDENS

Here, on 300 pretty, peaceful acres beside the river and Kew village, you can discover more than 30,000 species from the plant kingdom. In 2003 UNESCO named the garden a World Heritage Site for its contributions to science and its unique plant collections. Come early to make the most of your visit. The Victoria Gate Visitor Centre has guided and self-guided themed tours (for adults) and a special self-guided trail leaflet (for kids) that will get you tracking down plants and learning quirky facts about the conservatories. Guides are on hand to answer questions, too.

The gardens began in 1759 with the botanic collection of Augusta, the princess of Wales, on the grounds of Kew Palace. The collection grew, and wonderful garden buildings, such as the striking 10-story, red-gray brick Chinese Pagoda, were added. Other fabulous buildings followed. The huge Temperate House and Palm House conservatories, by Decimus Burton (of Hyde Park Arch fame), are lovely. Elevated areas let you climb up around the palms, and a marine section contains giant kelp, used in lipstick, toothpaste, and

EATS FOR KIDS The **Coffee Shop** in the Victoria Gate Visitor Centre sells filled baguettes, cakes, goodies, and coffee. **White Peaks** (closed in winter) has pizzas and other kids' favorites. The **Orangery** (020/8332–5186), an option for more sophisticated eating, is close to the main gate.

KEEP IN MIND Seasonal festivals and events celebrate the changes in the gardens—often focusing on themes of biodiversity—with lots of trails, quizzes, and fun facts on the fascinating flora. For one week in July the gardens play host to an outdoor music festival, but tickets sell fast, so check the Web site for details at least a couple of months in advance. The trip here from central London takes around 40 minutes.

Kew Rd., Kew. Tube: Kew Gardens.
Rail: Kew Bridge

 020/8332-5655;
www.kew.org

 £7.50 ages 17 and up,
children 16 and under free

Apr–Aug, M–F 9:30–6, Sa–Su 9:30–7;
Sept–Oct and Feb–Mar, daily 9:30–5;
Nov–Jan, daily 9:30–3:45

 All ages

ice cream. Bananas grow in the Palm House, as do cocoa trees, giant bamboo, and the super-climber Hairy Mary.

If you want to know how plants have shaped our world, stop by the Evolution House to study its early fossils. If dramatic and exotic is your thing, walk across the world's climatic zones in the Princess of Wales Conservatory; here you see prickly cacti, giant water lilies to rival Monet's, the carnivorous Venus flytrap, and plants that look like stones.

And that's just the indoor stuff. The buildings are mere dots on this broad landscape of interlinked formal gardens, arboretums, and woodland on the River Thames. You can run or meander, and as the seasons change, so does the scenery. Early spring brings carpets of purple crocuses; late spring sees fruit and other trees laden with blossoms. Summer is the time for the scent of roses and blooming water lilies as well as fun kids' activities that emphasize eco-friendliness. A garden is always full of surprises.

HEY, KIDS! The Venus flytrap, that most enterprising of plants, can also count. It efficiently snaps up its prey—flies and other small insects—when it has felt not one but two touches on the fine hairs inside its leaves. If you're lucky enough to see one of these amazing plants in action in the Princess of Wales Conservatory, you'll also discover that its fly-catching maneuver makes it the planet's plant sprinting champ.

ROYAL MEWS AT BUCKINGHAM PALACE

The Queen's palace is London's stateliest sight, with guards standing sentry inside the ornate black-and-gold gates (*see* Changing of the Guard). But equally impressive are the gilded coaches and elegant black carriages that sweep out majestically along the Mall with their horses and liveried coachmen on state and royal occasions. These glorious coaches are kept in the stable courtyard, or mews, at the side of the palace and can be seen along with some tack and the horses themselves.

The first stage of your visit passes the Riding School, where the horses are trained. It's a rigorous program that includes pulling broad, heavy weights and learning to keep cool while bands play and crowds wave flags and shout. Queen Victoria's young family of nine was schooled in riding here, but not the current princes William and Harry.

Next come the carriages, stationed outside each numbered door. They are decked in highly polished leather, red and gilt paint, and shiny brass lanterns and are quite high off the

KEEP IN MIND The State Rooms at Buckingham Palace are open to the public only when the Queen is out of town in the summer. Generally, this is during July and August. Tickets should be booked a month in advance by calling the visitor center number above. It's worth noting that although the decor and treasures on display are amazing for adults, they don't tend to interest kids as much. The Queen's Gallery (tel. 020/7321–2233), in the palace's former chapel, is a bit highbrow, but older kids may appreciate the portraits and Fabergé oddities, and perhaps the eclectic collection of drawings.

Buckingham Palace Rd., SW1.
Tube: Victoria

 £5 ages 17 and up,
£2.50 children 5–16

 Daily 11–3.15, until 4:15
Aug–Sept

020/7766–7302 or 020/7321–2233;
www.royal.gov.uk

5 and up

ground. So how does the Queen ascend regally? A swift response comes from one of the stewards: a footman unfolds steps from inside the carriage door. The Gold State Coach is the must-see masterpiece, almost completely gold with cherubs and two mythical Tritons on the back to scare off anyone racing up behind. These stately vehicles don't race, however. They proceed at walking pace, pulled by four pairs of horses with postilion riders and accompanying footmen, all in red-and-gold regalia. The Queen used the coach for her 1952 coronation, her 1977 Silver Jubilee, and her Golden Jubilee in 2002.

It's unlikely you'll catch the Queen in the stables, although she does name each horse herself. Her Majesty is an accomplished rider, and the beautiful little saddles used by the young princesses Elizabeth and Margaret are on exhibit in the Harness Room. One appears to be decorated with flowers; if you look close up, you'll see they are little shells sewn together.

HEY, KIDS! If you were wondering what the word "mews" means, it is from the French word *mue*, which means to shed an outer coat, or moult. In days of old, the word was used for the place where falcons were kept when they were shedding their feathers.

EATS FOR KIDS Head toward Victoria Street rather than Buckingham Palace Road for a better selection of coffee bars, such as **Starbucks** (137 Victoria St., tel. 020/7233–5170). The excellent **Spaghetti House** (3 Bressenden Pl., tel. 020/7834–5650) serves truly Italian pastas, pizza, and meat dishes in a friendly modern bistro setting. Smaller portions at reduced prices are available for kids.

ROYAL NATIONAL THEATRE

Here's a chance for young drama enthusiasts to go behind the scenes of one of Britain's most famous theaters—to see how it all works and learn the tricks of the trade. You never know what might happen; you might even brush past a great actor as you pass the dressing rooms.

A guide with an encyclopedic knowledge of plays past and forthcoming takes you into each of the three theaters that make up the National Theatre complex and explains the mechanics of each. Sitting in each one, perhaps catching part of a rehearsal, you discover how each one's shape and size are suited to specific types of performances.

Backstage areas are like vast warehouses. You see entire sets ready to be wheeled in and out, just like freight on rail tracks. Countless props and furniture pieces—even glitzy chandeliers dangling high in the rafters—are recycled time and again. Not only can you peek at the props, but you learn how they work and how they're made and hear fascinating

KEEP IN MIND In addition to the permanent theater-history exhibition in the Olivier Theatre, changing exhibitions of arts and crafts are presented in the vast foyer area. Throughout the summer, dance, mime, and music events are staged on the open-air riverside walk just outside the theater—all for free.

EATS FOR KIDS The theater contains **Mezzanine** (tel. 020/7452–3600), for fine dining; the **Terrace Café** (tel. 020/7452–3555), with grills, salads, and pastas; and the **Circle Cafe**, with the most family appeal. They open based on performances. **EAT** espresso bar has great coffee, pastries, and outdoor tables. **Lyttelton Buffet** has sandwiches and sweets. The **People's Palace** (Level 3, Royal Festival Hall, tel. 020/7928–9999) is a chic restaurant next door, and **La Barca** (81 Lower Marsh, tel. 020/7261–9221) is a cozy trattoria.

South Bank Centre, Belvedere Rd., SE1.
Tube: Waterloo

020/7452-3400;
www.nationaltheatre.org.uk

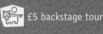
£5 backstage tour

M–Sa 3 times a day; tour times vary based on performances

8 and up

tales about their stage successes and disasters. For instance, you find out why there are three different huge but almost cuddly working crocodiles needed in *Peter Pan* and how the fake food for *Wind in the Willows* is made to look good enough to eat. (The Theatre Museum has an exhibition devoted to this production; *see #9*.) You even discover the secrets of how real-looking blood is made to spurt out at just the right second—well, sometimes it's been hit or miss. In the scenery-making area, you see the genius of the stage designers who turn bits of seeming garbage into realistic-looking sets. Green-painted raffia becomes stage grass; hard sponge turns to stone. You might even wonder if it's the set designers, rather than the actors, who are the real masters of disguise.

At tour's end you can follow a time line on the history of the theater, but more likely you'll be itching to reserve seats for the next sizzling performance, so you can see all that backroom work from the front.

HEY, KIDS! Even the cleverest stage props can go wrong. In one performance of *Peter Pan*, Smee, the pirate cook, had to improvise quickly when Captain Hook's hook suddenly shot out into the audience. He retrieved it. And in a grisly scene from *Macbeth*, a fake bloodied head was not made heavy enough. It ended up bouncing, like a ball, across the stage.

ROYAL OBSERVATORY

It's about time. The Greenwich observatory is synonymous with time and its connection with the Earth and sea. It was established in 1675 to help find a solution to the critical problem of calculating longitude (those thin, black, vertical lines that you see on globes), and thus location, at sea. Work by royal astronomers and decades of dogged effort by clockmaker John Harrison (1693–1776) produced a solution in the 18th century. The 0° longitude line—the prime meridian—was established at Greenwich in 1884 by international agreement. Greenwich Mean Time is based on this. Pause in the observatory courtyard to see the location of the meridian—shown as a brass line across the cobbles. A photo, legs astride the western and eastern hemispheres, is a must.

The small museum traces the history of astronomy and the search for navigational longitude. It's an absorbing place, and though far from interactive, it still interests kids who love planets, seafaring, and timekeeping. There are telescopes, clocks, chronometers, and other exquisite historical timepieces as well as exhibits charting discoveries by such royal

HEY, KIDS! The red ball on top of the observatory drops down the rod at 1 PM on the dot, just as it has every day since 1833. Sailors used this system to set their clocks precisely to Greenwich Mean Time. Before then, the sun and stars were used to measure latitude, but without an accurate onboard clock they couldn't determine their longitude. And without that knowledge, many a ship came to a horrible end, unable to find its destination precisely or on schedule. Boats were shipwrecked and crews starved all because sailors couldn't determine time and longitude accurately enough.

Greenwich Park, SE10.
Tube: Cutty Sark

020/8312-6575 voice, 020/8312-6565
recording, 020/8312-6608 planetarium;
www.nmm.ac.uk

 Observatory free; planetarium
shows £4 ages 16 and up,
£2 children 15 and under

 Observatory daily 10–5;
planetarium shows M–F 2:30,
3:30, but varies during year

10 and up

astronomers as John Flamsteed, after whom the building (designed by Christopher Wren) is named, and Edmund Halley, of comet fame. Among the treasures are the sea clocks, H-1 to H-5, that Harrison made to measure longitude away from land. To make sense of it all, check out the wall display and press the longitude lines to see how time changes around the world.

Too much street light and pollution forced the main Royal Observatory operations to move out of London, but you can still look through the camera obscura. With a small aperture in the roof, a mirror, a round table, and a completely dark room, it shows a 360° image of the outside world, in this case the National Maritime Museum (see #26). You can watch a star show in the domed planetarium, and on scheduled dates you can look through the huge refracting telescope to view planets with the help of an astronomer. As you leave, don't forget to check your watch by the grand old 24-hour clock still ticking away.

KEEP IN MIND

Greenwich makes a great outing, especially if maritime and historical sights appeal. Allow a day to see everything—particularly if you're taking time to come by boat from Westminster or Tower Pier. If the weather's fine, you'll want to explore Greenwich Park (see #50), too.

EATS FOR KIDS If you don't want to go far, the **Park Café** (see Greenwich Park), just opposite the observatory, is your best choice. Also nearby is the National Maritime Museum (see #26); you can eat in its restaurant. Another option is to browse around Greenwich center (see Cutty Sark) and see what you like. In fine weather, purchase picnic fixings and explore Greenwich Park to find a choice sport for your meal.

ST. PAUL'S CATHEDRAL

I t may have the world's third-largest dome, but this was actually Christopher Wren's *smaller* design to replace the cathedral destroyed in the Great Fire of 1666. St. Paul's took more than 35 years to build and still dominates London's skyline, having survived the bombs of World War II. It has been the setting for momentous ceremonies, such as the wedding of Diana and Charles.

Before you tackle the sweeping front steps, look for the fun children's guidebook sold in the crypt shop, which contains key facts, highlights, and quizzes. Then head for the quire (choir) and high altar, and crane your neck to see the bright mosaics of heavenly images. In contrast to Westminster Abbey, St. Paul's is spacious and relatively simple; Wren wanted to keep the clutter of memorials and monuments in the crypt. But do visit the American Chapel, dedicated to the 28,000 GIs who died during World War II while serving in Britain or en route to the country.

HEY, KIDS!

While creating the dome murals, artist James Thornhill stepped back from his rope platform to admire his work and almost fell off, but his quick-thinking assistant grabbed him in time. Though it left a blotch, a life was saved. Can you spot where?

EATS FOR KIDS Beneath the beautiful arches, the **Crypt Café** (020/7246–8358) offers a children's menu with mozzarella pizza or chicken fingers served with ice cream and a drink. Smart choices for adults include a chicken niçoise salad (with olives and anchovies) and herbed haddock fish cakes with vegetable sides (allow around £10). For french fries in a French-style bar-bistro and substantial steak or chicken baguettes that children can share (from £6.95), try the aptly named **Café Dôme** (4 St. Paul's Churchyard, tel. 020/7489–0767). Opposite the cathedral, it has a wonderful view of the facade.

St. Paul's Churchyard, EC4.
Tube: Cannon St., St. Paul's

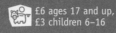 £6 ages 17 and up,
£3 children 6–16

 Cathedral M–Sa 8:30–4; galleries
M–Sa 9:30–4:15

020/7236–4128;
www.stpauls.co.uk

5 and up

Climb the 259 steps to the Whispering Gallery to see the dome, painted with sepia murals of St. Paul. You're now 100 feet above the floor, and you can stand against the wall and whisper a message to someone standing a distance away, who may hear your echo—hopefully distinct from everyone else's. The interior dome is smaller than the exterior one and 60 feet lower; between the two a brick cone supports the 850-ton lantern, surmounted by its golden ball and cross. For the ultimate stair-climbing challenge—another 368 steps, or 627 total— and assuming you have a head for heights, climb the spiraling grated stairs to the Golden Gallery, in the open air, on top of the dome. The view stretches for miles, taking in the graceful Millennium Bridge and the river bend that makes Big Ben look as if it's leaped to the South Bank.

Downstairs in the crypt are the grandiose tombs of Admiral Nelson and the duke of Wellington, as well as the simple plaque for Wren himself, who didn't live to see his great work finished. His Latin memorial states: "If you seek his monument, look around you."

KEEP IN MIND You'll need strong, stable shoes for walking up to the Whispering Gallery, and strong, stable legs and nerves to attempt the stairs to the balustrade outside the dome. (Older kids may well love that final climb, though.) The Triforium Tour takes you to parts of the cathedral not open to the public with general admission, including the library, Wren's great model of the cathedral, and another bunch of stairs: the Geometrical (or Dean's) Staircase. This tour runs on Mondays and Thursdays and costs £10, including cathedral admission.

SCIENCE MUSEUM

Eyes and minds open wide in this museum's popular, souped-up Wellcome Wing, an undeniably cool place with blue lighting and a sci-fi lab atmosphere. What makes it—and the rest of the museum, for that matter—even cooler is that the hands-on exhibits here are related to everyday things. After a visit, kids won't think of science as just space travel and DNA.

There are more than 800 exhibits to try here, so physical and mental stamina (not to mention plenty of time) are musts. Head for one of the touch-screen terminals by the main stairs and elevators for suggested itineraries (e.g., In a Hurry for Families and What to Do in Two Hours or Less). Or just stay in the Wellcome Wing. The tiniest visitors can learn how basic science works at Launch Pad, where they can press, push, pull, or play with sand and water while learning about light, sound, and electricity. Older kids (around 10–13) like the In the Future gallery, where computers let them enter their opinions about such topics as picking the sex of your child, men having babies, and growing young, and then find out

HEY, KIDS! Next time you miss a day at school, why not pick up a few new excuses from the Who Am I? exhibit, which explores some of the strange genetic diseases you just may have inherited—for the day? You could try telling your friends that you had a tiny case of didaskaleinophobia, and see if they know the meaning (a fear of going to school). Or how about decidophobia (a fear of making decisions)? And as for the dreaded visit to the dentist, well, there's always a sudden instance of iatrophobia.

Exhibition Rd., SW7.
Tube: South Kensington

Free; IMAX £7.50 ages 17 and up,
£4.95 children 5–16; charges for
special exhibitions

Daily 10–6

0870/870–4868;
www.sciencemuseum.org.uk

3 and up

what other kids think. In Who Am I? you can explore genetics with a little button pushing and discover how you got those distinguishing features. After all the interactive games, kids can sit back and enjoy the 3-D IMAX presentations, in which you get to wear those funny specs and experience virtual reality, such as visit to a space station.

Other galleries contain gorgeous vintage engines from the Victorian age, with engineers on hand to explain their workings. For those who just want to have fun, there's a virtual ride to Mars and more, near the Flight Lab. Kids interested in how flight evolved can try some hands-on experiments, such as hair-raising wind tunnels. Still have energy? Special exhibitions cover current topics. A recent James Bond show displayed some of the movies' hottest props, such as the Aston Martin Vanquish. Now that's where gizmos come in handy.

KEEP IN MIND
To help you plan your itinerary, notice the hand symbols on the museum map (indicating hands-on galleries) as well as the times of demonstrations, performances, and workshops. Note that children under 12 must be accompanied by an adult in the Launch Pad.

EATS FOR KIDS You will be much too busy exploring and interacting to leave the museum, so you might as well plunge into the high-tech-design **Deep Blue Café**, on the ground floor. A children's menu consists of chicken nuggets, mini pizza, or pasta plus dessert and drink; other options are rotisserie chicken and fries, pizzas, and salads. The self-serve **Museum Café** sells lunch and snacks in less chic surroundings, and the **Eat Drink Shop** is basic self-serve with hot dogs, sandwiches, cakes, ices, and candy bars.

SHAKESPEARE'S GLOBE

On the bank of the Thames, under bundles of water reeds and surrounded by English oak, William Shakespeare's artistic home has risen again. The Globe was the persistent dream of the late American actor and director Sam Wanamaker, who tried to find Shakespeare's London theater in 1949. All that was left of it then was a plaque on the wall of a brewery, but through his efforts the Globe was reborn in 1996, just a few hundred yards from its original foundations and a few centuries after its 1600s heyday. Your admission to the Globe's exhibition includes a tour of the theater (if a performance is not in progress).

From the moment you walk into the open-air theater, you enter a time warp. As guides explain, few concessions to modern technology were made in its construction. Everything was done by hand, without electricity, as in Shakespeare's day; there's not a screw in sight. Those water reeds make the only thatched roof in London, as such roofs were banned after the Great Fire. Oak forms the supports, seats, and stage. Performances use original methods, too, with no microphones or lighting. Music is provided by lutes, pipes, drums, and

HEY, KIDS!
The Globe is shaped like a wooden "O." Pay more for a ticket and you can sit underneath the circular thatched roof. The audience members in the center, called groundlings, have no roof, and they stand. If it rains, they get wet; the show goes on.

KEEP IN MIND If you want to get a taste of the real thing—and perhaps be a groundling—attend one of several special matinees during the summer theater season. Running concurrently with these is ChildsPlay, the ultimate in cultural baby-sitting. While parents enjoy a performance, their children attend this workshop (£10), which zooms in on bite-size sections of the play and sparks their imagination through drama, story-telling, and art. Kids then watch the last 20 minutes in the theater. Are your kids ready for a full play? Check out kids' discounts and note that performance schedules vary.

21 New Globe Walk, Bankside, SE1.
Tube: London Bridge

020/7902–1500;
www.shakespeares-globe.org

Exhibition £8 ages 16 and up,
£5.50 children 5–15; performances:
groundlings £5, seats from £13 ages
16 and up

Exhibition May–Sept, daily 9–5;
Oct–Apr, daily 10–5; theater
season May–Sept

8 and up

other instruments of the time—you can see them in the theater's exhibition—and actors stroll from stage to audience as the play demands. When cannon fire was needed for *Henry V,* the *Golden Hinde* replica, just along the riverbank, obliged.

The largest exhibit of its kind in the world, Shakespeare's Globe Exhibition celebrates the Bard's plays—from Dame Judi Dench to Disney—and includes gorgeous handmade costumes. It also covers the drama of how craftspeople built the theater as well as archaeological finds, among them a child's tiny leather shoes. Demonstrations of costume making or sword fighting often take place in the exhibition. Drawings, paintings, and diary entries show that Southwark (a.k.a. the South Bank), with its playhouses, alehouses, and bear dancing, was London's playground in the days of the original Globe. When the Puritan regime closed the theaters in 1642, the area died with it. Today, thanks to Sam Wanamaker, the Tate Modern, and the Millennium Bridge, Southwark is enjoying a renaissance.

EATS FOR KIDS The **Globe Café** (tel. 020/7902–1576) serves lunch, brunch, and snacks; sandwiches and soup are pricey, at £3.75 and £6.95, but they come with a beautiful view over the theater piazza and the Millennium Bridge and across the river to St. Paul's Cathedral. For other dining suggestions, see *Golden Hinde,* Tate Modern, and Millennium Bridge.

SOMERSET HOUSE

One of London's architectural treasures, the 18th-century, riverside Somerset House has squeezed out the dreary offices that were once here and opened its front and back doors to the public. The front (Strand) entrance brings you to the Courtauld Gallery (see #55), with its fine art collection; the back (Embankment) leads to the Gilbert Collection of decorative arts. Between them is an elegant courtyard reminiscent of an Italian palazzo, and though the Courtauld and the Gilbert Collection are worth separate visits, the rest of Somerset House is a fun place to spend an hour or two.

The most exciting way to arrive is by foot from Waterloo Bridge. You can imagine how London was in the 18th century, when the river lapped Venetian-style at the building's water-gate entrance and Navy Board barges (the navy had offices here) arrived from Greenwich. You can see the Commissioners' Barge at the old river level, beneath the Great Arch, bearing the face of Old Father Thames. (The busy embankment road was built a century later.) A huge video that plays on the entrance-lobby wall tells the house's history, and around the

EATS FOR KIDS The Admiralty Deli, in Seaman's Hall, sells snacks and drinks to eat in the courtyard. To sit on the river terrace you have to eat at the sophisticated, pricey **Admiralty** (tel. 020/7845–4646) restaurant. More fun is had on the far side of Covent Garden, at **Belgo** (50 Earlham St., tel. 020/7813–2233), a weird techno monastery (waiters wear funky monk outfits) where kids can color before plunging into fabulous Belgian *frites* (fries), with crumbed chicken or fish. Parents make do with mussels stuffed with savory mixtures, washed down with fruity beers. See also Courtauld Gallery and Covent Garden.

Strand, WC2. Tube: Covent Garden, Holborn, Waterloo

 020/7845–4600; www.somerset-house.org.uk

 Free

M–Sa 10–6, Su 12–6

6 and up

corner, the education room hosts practical activities, such as mask making and other crafts. (Younger children must be accompanied by an adult.) For a thought-provoking self-guided tour, pick up a free family guide sheet, which gets you hunting around the river terrace, Seaman's Hall, and courtyard for interesting objects.

The courtyard is the hub for a huge range of activities on many weekends, particularly in summer: free music performances, mimes, and more to watch, plus children's art projects, such as scrap sculpture, and other crafts to join in for as little or as much time as you want. A quarterly events sheet gives full details. While you watch today's activity, realize that beneath your feet lie the remains of the Tudor palace built by the duke of Somerset, which was torn down in 1775. Just imagine how the royal jester might have entertained the future Queen Elizabeth I, who once lived here.

HEY, KIDS! Admiral Nelson, an important figure on the Navy Board, reported regularly to Somerset House. Although his character looms large, as the family guide sheet describes, he was actually "a thin, spare naval officer with only one arm . . . His frail figure shook at every step."

KEEP IN MIND Drop-in workshops for children run 11:30–1 and 2–4; phone ahead for dates and details or check the "What's On" leaflet at the admission desk. Guided tours that include the Gilbert Collection (£5) run Tuesdays, Thursdays, and Saturdays at 1:30 and take 1 hour and 15 minutes; tours that include the Courtauld Gallery (£5) start at 3:15 on those same days. For more fun in December and January, the courtyard is transformed into an ice-skating rink (with a Christmas tree in season). Tickets (0870/166–0423) are popular, so book in advance; the Web site has information.

SYON PARK

Despite the overhead rumble of jets from nearby Heathrow Airport, Syon Park has 55 acres of beautiful, peaceful gardens rolling down to the River Thames. Home of the dukes of Northumberland for more than 400 years, Syon has had gardens since 1431, when it was a medieval abbey. After it became a ducal residence, the gardens were redesigned on a grand scale by Capability (Lancelot) Brown, the must-have gardener of the 18th century.

As you enter, you come to the most eye-catching feature: the Great Conservatory. Made by Charles Fowler, who also designed the old flower market at Covent Garden, it is filled with plants, many of which have interesting tales relating to their arrival from some exotic corner of the globe. Your kids might want to run from one end to the other or in circles around the pretty fountain in the garden behind. From here a path leads to the rose garden and Syon House itself. You can sneak a peek inside the grand entrance; even children are in awe of the gorgeous high, decorated ceilings. While you stroll and breathe in the delicate scents of the rose garden, your kids can race between the beds.

HEY, KIDS!

Henry VIII's coffin lay here overnight on its way from Westminster to Windsor for burial, but in the morning the coffin was found open and dogs were licking the remains. Could it be divine retribution because Henry closed the abbey that once stood on the grounds?

KEEP IN MIND On the Syon estate but a separate enterprise, the indoor adventure playground Snakes and Ladders (tel. 020/8847–0946), designed for tiny tots and young kids up to 10 (the height limit is 4 feet, 8 inches), will prove a magnet if the weather's bad. It's open daily 10–6 and costs from £5 per child on weekends, £3.15 weekdays. Also on the Syon grounds are Aquatic Experience (see #68) and London Butterfly House (see #39).

London Rd., Brentford.
Tube: Gunnersbury

020/8560-0881;
www.syonpark.co.uk

£3.50 ages 15 and up,
£2.50 children 5-14

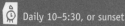
Daily 10-5:30, or sunset

3 and up

Around the conservatory, proud peacocks strut about, showing off their plumage—a great photo op—and warning you to keep your distance with their eerie shrieks. On weekends you can catch a miniature steam railway, which trundles past a lake to Flora's Lawn, a lovely picnic and game-playing spot. On a pretty walk beside the lake you might see all sorts of ducks, their nests hidden in the reeds. Look out for many unusual trees, too. Syon has a diverse collection, and some, like the Indian bean, whose tangled trunk snakes along the ground, are a dream for kids to climb. Take the footbridge and path toward the tidal water meadows (also the site of a Civil War battle in 1642), and observe the Thames and its bobbing boats and chic waterside houses.

If it rains, you might tempt your kids into the stately house. Although its core is Tudor, most of the house is Georgian, by Robert Adam, the sought-after 18th-century architect and decorator. But likely as not, kids will want to explore the outdoor space of this idyllic place.

EATS FOR KIDS Since it's quite a way to get off-site, you are pretty much a captive audience. The self-service **Patio Café**, at the park entrance, serves many child-friendly dishes (pastas, sausages, and chicken, to name a few), snacks, and drinks. You can bring your own picnic to the park, but first fill your picnic bag at the **Syon Park Farm Shop**, near the parking lot, which has some unusual organic English produce and a good deli.

TATE BRITAIN

Just because the current fuss is about Tate Modern (and justifiably so—*see #11*), downriver, don't pass Tate Britain by. Now that the international pictures that were once here have emigrated to the South Bank, the greatest collection of British art anywhere, from 1500 to today, can be seen in bright and spacious surroundings. The gallery has taken the bold step of arranging works thematically. Your family can walk into a room called The Portrait and enjoy wildly different styles from different centuries hanging in the same space. Compare the formal 18th-century painting of the *Bishop of Winchester*, by William Hogarth, with Peter Blake's pioneering Pop Art *Self-Portrait with Badges*, from 1961. This kind of juxtaposition continues throughout the gallery and covers other subjects, such as war, land, and home life. The result is a fun, new perspective on art.

Come on a Sunday afternoon, 2–5, when the kids' Art Trolley is wheeled out. From it children can collect materials, head for a designated work (perhaps David Hockney's *Bigger Splash*), set themselves up on the floor, and make their own work of art. There are other activity choices, too, and the trolley is updated regularly to reflect the galleries' changing displays. Older kids often work quietly on their own, allowing you to take an uninterrupted look at the paintings by yourself without anyone getting frustrated.

The information desk dispenses audio guides as well as special kids' work sheets based on different themes relating to animals, family life, or emotions. Armed with pencil and clipboard, children head off for works around the gallery. Suitable for a wide age range, the sheets get them to think about what is happening in each piece and to compare art from different times. The sheets also suggest ways for kids to write or draw their impressions. In a sheet identifying different dads, for example, the 1636 picture of *The Saltonstall Family* is in stark contrast to 1978's *Melanie & Me Swimming,* though in some ways they are very similar. Older kids might navigate the Tate's excellent Web site before heading off to hot spots such as Bridget Riley's mesmerizing wavy lines.

KEEP IN MIND

Those still in an art frenzy can cruise by boat to Tate Modern downriver on the South Bank. The Tate to Tate service runs every 40 minutes during gallery hours. Get tickets from the information desk or call 020/7887–8888.

HEY, KIDS! The two biggest geniuses of British landscape painting (works showing natural scenery) are generally considered to be John Constable and J. M. W. Turner. You can find the world's best collection of their works here, in the Clore Gallery. They both painted in the early 19th century, but what is even more surprising is that they both chose to focus many of their paintings on the same picturesque part of England—the counties of Norfolk and Suffolk, known collectively as East Anglia. Constable produced rural country scenes, while Turner favored the vibrant colors of sunsets and seascapes.

TATE MODERN

As art galleries go, this is the best for kids. The building once housed a power station, and in its modernistic, high-tech conversion the central space was kept in its original massive proportions—great for displaying large, towering, wacky pieces of sculpture. Just walking in gives you the sense that anything can happen, and, as you soon discover at this off-the-wall, modern-art museum, it does.

You can choose from several children's programs. Kids like the audio trail, which explores selected pieces in the landscape gallery, from Richard Long's ring of red granite stones on the gallery floor and his photos of fields of daisies to Claude Monet's Impressionist lily pond. You might think these are miles apart, but both have similar aims. Poems, music, and artists' and kids' points of view—no arty-speak here—prompt children to look at art in fun ways, determine their own opinions, and really get involved. They also learn about techniques created by groundbreaking artists as they look at Henri Matisse's snail collage and Jackson Pollock's squiggles. Not only do kids find these pieces wild and attractive,

KEEP IN MIND Starters is a free, innovative workshop run by artists for kids 5 and up accompanied by an adult. The workshops are offered every Saturday afternoon at 2, as well as on other days during vacations. Check with the information desk for details.

EATS FOR KIDS The spacious **Café** (Level 2, tel. 020/7401–5413), actually on the ground floor, has floor-to-ceiling windows overlooking the river and St. Paul's Cathedral. The British-accented menu includes seasonal dishes—light grills with salads in summer, casseroles and root-vegetable mash (mashed potatoes) in winter—followed by British cheeses or to-die-for desserts. Children find plenty of pastas and meat dishes. Alternatively, pick up picnic supplies from the **Espresso Bar** (Level 4) or **Jan's** (59 Upper Ground, tel. 020/7928–6450), at Hatfields and Upper Ground. Also see *Golden Hinde*, Millennium Bridge, and Shakespeare's Globe.

25 Sumner St., Bankside, SE1.
Tube: Blackfriars, London Bridge, Southwark

 Free

Su-Th 10–6, F–Sa 10–10

020/7887–8008; www.tate.org.uk

7 and up

they are encouraged to think about what the artist might (or might not) have been trying to achieve. Parents can join in the fun, too.

Start is a program specifically for families looking around the gallery together. Pick up a map and a bag of games and puzzles on Level 3, and set off on your journey. You can take as little or as much time as you want, but when you've finished, you can stick your impressions and drawings on the wall—actually having your work hung in one of the world's largest modern-art galleries. If you'd rather take your work and ideas away with you, try the Explorers family trails, available from the information desk. These focus on small sections of the gallery; you might make your own time capsule, for instance, or be an art critic, with help from a folder that suggests different viewpoints. Whatever you do, you'll find your trip here explores art at its interactive and thoughtful best.

HEY, KIDS! While the building was being renovated, workers would arrive in the morning to be greeted by a family of foxes that had made their home in the disused power station—quite a strange sight in this urban area. The foxes were given an alternative home, but pigeons refused to leave. The birds have become even more of a problem now that thousands of visitors leave crumbs outside. On most Fridays, long before visitors arrive, a black hawk (kept especially for the job) is let out on the roof to scare the pesky pigeons and keep them from making a permanent roost.

For maximum impact, arrive by boat to appreciate the great hulk that is the Thames Barrier, an amazing structure resembling a set of humongous, shiny steel shells positioned in a defensive line across the river. It's defensive not in the military sense but because London has recorded "gret wyndes and fluddes" as far back as 1099. In 1236 you could actually row a boat inside Westminster Hall. Water levels have risen each century, but a greater problem is surge tides, which occur when the North Sea rises and increases the tidal flow of the Thames estuary. Such a disaster occurred in 1953; more than 300 people were drowned and 165,000 acres of farmland were flooded. A barrier became necessary, and the radical radial gate design was completed in 1984.

In the visitor center, start with a film that describes the history in lively detail, with fabulous fire and water effects that appear to engulf the stage. With history pumping in your brain, find out all there is to know about the river's life and how the barrier was conceived and engineered through yet another film, in a small but intensively interactive exhibit area.

EATS FOR KIDS The **Riverside Terrace Café** (tel. 020/8854–8028) sells sandwiches, ices, and snacks, but if you want a bigger refuel and greater options, go to Greenwich, home to riverside pubs, village restaurants, museums, and the *Cutty Sark* (see #53). Thames Path walkers are amply rewarded at the cozy, nautical, 200-year-old **Cutty Sark** (Ballast Quay, tel. 020/8858–3146), a pub at journey's end. The eponymous ship is a good ½ mile farther. Tables practically on the river have wonderful views across to Canary Wharf and the Docklands, and food includes stuffed Yorkshire puddings.

1 Unity Way, Woolwich, SE18.
Rail: Charlton

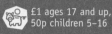 £1 ages 17 and up,
50p children 5–16

Apr–Sept, daily 10:30–4:30;
Oct–Mar, daily 11–3:30

020/8305–4188;
www.environment-agency.gov.uk

4 and up

Play with telephones that serve as a mock barrier control center, and turn handles and push buttons to discover more about the river and its diverse life—from salmon to mollusks—an improvement since 1962, when the river was so polluted that nothing survived in it. An artificial smell gives a hint of how nasty it could get back in 1856, before there were sewage systems. A computer section follows the history of Old Father Thames and other aspects of life on the riverbank.

By now you'll want to get onto one of the barrier pier sections, but, due to security, that's not possible. The best way to get close is to take one of the frequent boats from Greenwich or Westminster that pass between the piers. Still, the view from the riverside shows the powerful industrial architecture—particularly if you walk a little upstream—and a good playground and picnic area on the grassy riverbank looks out on boats passing through the barrier and airplanes landing at City Airport, on the opposite shore.

HEY, KIDS! Want to know what it was like for the diving engineers who worked on the riverbed building the barrier's foundations? Jump inside the large white square cell in the mini playground. Then imagine it shut and surrounded by the pressure of the water. Feeling comfortable?

KEEP IN MIND Campion Launches (tel. 020/8305–0300) operates 30-minute boat trips to the barrier from Greenwich Pier, late February–late October. Service from Westminster via Canary Wharf is run by Thames Cruises (tel. 020/7930–3373). Both operators give accompanying tour commentary. The barrier marks the eastern end of the Thames Path (see Museum in Docklands), an alternative route back to Greenwich; allow about an hour for the walk. The route is marked by easy-to-see black signposts; check www.nationaltrails.gov.uk to see the entire trail of some 50 miles.

THEATRE MUSEUM

9

Not only can you learn all about the performing arts here, you can also experience them, as you get a glimpse of the world behind the scenes of a theater. In fact, the museum's warren-like corridors are just like being in an old West End theatre, with walls of vintage posters, programs, and signed photos of actors and dancers. A half-hour tour (offered throughout the day) charts the history of the British stage—its artists and famous shows—from Shakespeare to the grand actors Henry Irving and Sarah Bernhardt. The high point for kids is the video and exhibit on *The Wind in the Willows* by the Royal National Theatre (*see #19*), showing how actors metamorphose into a gang of sleazy, double-dealing stoats and weasels: the skill is in the flick of the head, the curl of the lip, the slide-skip walk, and the cockney accent. It's utterly convincing.

Kids will want to get into the act, so check at the entrance for the day's events. In some sessions, stage makeup artists will create any fantasy face you want. Meanwhile, you

HEY, KIDS!
Remember the tale of Tom Thumb? He was a real person: an American-born midget who used to entertain Queen Victoria. The museum has the teeny, elaborate waistcoat he used to wear and a picture of him performing on a table at a party.

EATS FOR KIDS Tuttons (11–12 Russell St., tel. 020/7836–4141), facing Covent Garden Piazza, has a brasserie menu with steak, Thai chicken, club sandwiches, fries, and fab desserts. Smaller portions of most dishes are available for kids on request. In summer, sit outside and watch the street musicians and passersby. **Maxwell's** (8–9 James St., tel. 020/7836–0303), opposite the museum, serves up burgers plus. For a British, no-frills filling meal, walk north on Bow Street to **Rock and Sole Plaice** (47 Endell St., tel. 020/7836–3785); fish-and-chips have been sold on this site for more than 100 years. Also see Covent Garden.

7 Russell St, WC2. Tube: Covent Garden

 Free

 T–Su 10–6 (last admission 5:30)

 020/7943–4700;
www.theatremuseum.org

6 and up

can watch a video that shows how the gruesome makeup for *Phantom of the Opera* is layered on. Now imagine singing with all that hardened goo around your mouth. Your youngster might also be able to take part in a dress-up session, using theatrical costumes from the small studio theater. On the less showy side, you can find out about early Chinese shadow puppetry, watch a little puppet performance, and then discover how to make your own small theater and puppets.

Stage Truck, a program of themed activities (usually connected with the long-running special exhibition on the museum's ground floor, which is worth a look), runs each Saturday and on weekdays during summer vacation. It's a must for budding performers eager to pick up tricks of the trade. Even cooler is the (free) Kids Theatre Club. Pitched to 8- to 12-year-olds, the program is where they get to work in sessions with real actors. Places are limited, so book well in advance for your thespian.

KEEP IN MIND Stage Truck runs during summer vacation, late July–early September, and kids under 12 must be accompanied by an adult. For younger kids, there are regular storytelling sessions. Call the museum or check the Web site for details. The National Video Archive also resides at the museum; to book your own front row seat to watch a screening of classic works by playwrights such as David Hare and Tom Stoppard in the Study Room, or to book a place in the Kids Theatre Club, call 020/7943–4806.

THORPE PARK

For the wildest way to get all shook up and wet west of London, hop on this series of rides that suit all ages and inclinations, from hardened thrill-riders to timids and tinies. Even if you spend all day here, you won't cover everything.

On the wet side, the highlight is the Tidal Wave, a huge water slide dominating the center of the park. It's imaginatively set in a fishing village in New England about to experience a freak disaster, but the slide looks more frightening than it is. Among the dry runs to assault your senses, Pirates 4-D is a swashbuckling film show with fantastic 3-D special effects. If you can't stand the sensation of bats or insects flapping in your face, loud sounds, and a vibrating floor, avoid it. It's all surreal and, despite the hammy acting, immense fun. The other mindblower is the ride called X:\No Way Out. After wandering through dimly lit tunnels, including a revolving neon drum with disorienting lighting and sound effects, you are thrown into a journey through the night sky. The very weird and sensational ride makes you feel lost in space, so it's not recommended for the nervous (or after a big lunch). Also

KEEP IN MIND Wise kids wear their swimming gear underneath light clothes that dry quickly after a soaking. Of course, if the weather's nice and warm, who cares about getting (and staying) wet? For those who don't like getting drenched, cheap waterproof ponchos are on sale. Since tickets are expensive and the park is large, you should arrive early to make the most of your day and avoid the lines for the popular rides, which get longer as the day progresses. Need help choosing what to do? With grades from "young adventurers" to "extreme," the Thrillometer is a good way to rate the rides.

Staines Rd., Chertsey, Surrey

 0870/444-4466;
www.thorpepark.com

 From £19 ages 12 and up, £15.50
children 4–11, children 3 and under
free; varies by season

Apr–Nov, M–F 10–6, later in
summer and on weekends

3 and up

in the scream-inducing category is Nemesis Inferno, which claims to be the world's most disorienting ride. Hardened, white-knuckle riders can judge after being whizzed around a full 360°, among other sense-adjusting drops and jerks. Quantum starts off slow and then churns you up and about. After these, you can catch your breath by watching someone else whirling in the Spider Man Stunt Show.

By comparison, Neptune's Beach offers plain water fun without fear. To dry out and slow down the pace, take the train ride over to Thorpe Farm, where you can pet the animals and then take a boat ride back. Adults and observant older kids may find that some of the older-style rides seem a little tame, but that's fine for family fun. And if the usual volume of kids' screams is anything to go by, there's obviously enough shriekable stuff for everyone.

EATS FOR KIDS
Unless you bring your own picnic (and there are many places to enjoy it), you'll have to choose from chain everything, from **Burger King** and **KFC** to **Donuts**; **Costa Coffee** and **Caffé Nero** are upscale coffee bars.

GETTING THERE Thorpe Park is off the M25 freeway, which loops around London. Take Exit 11 or 13 (not 12, as this puts you onto another freeway), and follow the signs. The entrance is off the A320 trunk road. By rail, catch a train from Waterloo Station to Staines. From there it's a short taxi ride (10 minutes) or a half-hour walk. The drive and train ride from central London are each about 40 minutes.

TOWER BRIDGE EXPERIENCE

Here's one of those landmarks that's a magnet for every tourist, but few realize they can walk inside it to discover how the bridge is raised. It's a fun, short visit that will appeal to kids who like machinery, and the rest of the family should enjoy the bridge if for nothing more than the spectacular views from the walkway between the two towers.

To unravel the bridge's story from the beginning—including some history of the river— follow the special route with videos and touch screens. Tower Bridge was constructed in 1894, when the Port of London was thriving and large trading ships came up the river to unload their goods. The design had to allow for river traffic, the increasing number of vehicles that were passing between the north and south banks, and pedestrians. The answer was a liftable "bascule" (drawbridge) design that had a pedestrian walkway beneath the spires of the two towers, which house the massive machinery. In the engine rooms (visited at the end of the tour) beneath the south tower on the south bank you can see the preserved steam-powered hydraulics that operated until 1976; electric controls are now used.

HEY, KIDS!
Imagine an airplane flying underneath the high-level walkway! It happened once. Luckily, no one was hurt, but not surprisingly the reckless pilot lost his job—even though he had mangaed to pull off the stunt.

KEEP IN MIND The royal yacht *Britannia* passed through the lifted bridge on its last voyage, and though you'll never see that sight again, you can still see the bridge lifted regularly. To find out if an opening might coincide with your itinerary, call 020/ 7378–7700 for information on the upcoming week. In summer and during other school vacations, free crafts workshops for kids are offered. One such is kite making—what better place to fly a kite than by the river! Combination tickets with the Monument (see #32) are available.

Tower Bridge, SE1.
Tube: Tower Hill

020/7403-3761;
www.towerbridge.org.uk

£4.50 ages 16 and up,
£4.25 children 5-15

Daily 9:30-5.30 (last admission 5)

6 and up

Hands-on exhibits demonstrate how the whole thing swings into life, with gears, spans, and huge, shiny cylinders. Thanks to the interactive displays and film, you won't get your hands dirty, unlike the original engine-room workers who kept the power stoked with coal.

Between the exhibits is the enclosed, high-level walkway, 140 feet above the river. It was designed to remain open while the bridge lifts; amazingly, this occurs up to 900 times a year. Computer displays along your route pick out key buildings on the skyline (smaller kids need a boost to get a view). To the east are modern superstructures like Canary Wharf, and to the west you get a great look at the steel-and-glass mushroom that is the Greater London Assembly's City Hall, the Tower of London, St. Paul's, and the Monument. Photographs show the area's changes over the years, and no doubt a return visit will reveal even more, since Thames-side development keeps powering ahead.

EATS FOR KIDS South of the river, set among very upscale restaurants in design-conscious Butlers Wharf, **Ask** (Butlers Wharf, tel. 020/7403–4545) serves pastas in smaller child's portions (from £3.50) and pizzas in the usual size (from £4.30). Along with the food you get great river views and the modern, streamlined, chrome surroundings so prevalent in Italian eateries. In summer you can sit outside. Also see Tower of London.

TOWER OF LONDON

"S end him to the Tower!" That royal command filled many a prisoner with dread, and those who entered by Traitors' Gate, on the Thames, were unlikely to return. The Tower actually comprises many different towers, added through the centuries. It has been a fortress, medieval palace, royal prison, and even the royal menagerie, the basis for the London Zoo. The original White Tower was built by the French duke William the Conqueror, who had it constructed to impress the locals; 900 years later it impresses tourists.

The Crown Jewels are a more modern addition (from 1660), but their splendor is no less staggering, as lines testify. Head to the Jewel House first; once through the thick strong-room doors, you watch a film of historic coronations. Then it's on to the real things: crowns bursting with jewels, scepters, rings, and other priceless paraphernalia whose diamonds are the size of minimuffins. The Queen's Imperial State Crown and scepter (with the world's largest cut diamond) are used each November for the State Opening of Parliament. To find out how they were made, visit the Martin Tower's Crowns and Diamonds exhibit.

KEEP IN MIND To avoid lining up for tickets, buy them from any Underground station or purchase them by phone or online. Another way to miss the worst crowds is to arrive early. (Allow at least three hours to explore.) At the entrance, pick up a children's work sheet (available during school vacations) and check the schedule of daily events and guided Yeoman Warder tours. These centuries-old guards (also called Beefeaters) wearing red-and-gold uniforms generally lead tours daily (subject to weather) and at no charge; tours leave from the Middle Tower about every 30 minutes until 3:30 in summer, 2:30 in winter.

Tower Hill, EC3.
Tube: Tower Hill

 0870/756-6060 information,
0870/756-7070 tickets;
www.hrp.org.uk

Advance tickets £12 ages 16
and up, £7.80 children 5-15;
gate prices £13.50 and £9

Mar-Oct, M-Sa 9-5; Su 10-5;
Nov-Feb, T-Sa 9-4; Su-M 10-4;
last entry 1 hr before closing

 5 and up

Aristocratic traitors were imprisoned in the Beauchamp Tower, where they killed time chiseling artistic graffiti in the walls. Only lords and ladies were beheaded here, and they're listed behind the executioner's block on Tower Green. The headless ghost of Anne Boleyn, Henry VIII's second wife, is said to walk by with her entourage. To get an idea of what life was like, go to the Wakefield Tower, where costumed guides answer questions and tell tales of those sometimes terrible times. Weapons fanatics find the elaborate displays of flintlock pistols and swords in the White Tower absorbing. Check out the armor, particularly Henry VIII's extra-extra-large size and miniversions for little princes, and the old arsenal, where gunpowder barrels line the walls. Thankfully, the Great Fire of 1666, which started in the nearby City, stopped short of the Tower; if it hadn't, London would have had a truly explosive fireworks show and we would have been deprived of this fascinating glimpse into the past.

EATS FOR KIDS
The **New Armouries Restaurant** serves fresh food and traditional recipes courtesy of chef Digby Trout. The interior looks much like the original horse armory. Outside the tower, two **Pret a Manger** stands sell good sandwiches and snacks, but you may have to fight off some hungry pigeons.

HEY, KIDS! The Tower has ghost stories and legends galore. The tale of the young Princes Edward and Richard, who died in 1483, is the saddest one. The story goes that they stand holding hands in their nightgowns before fading into the walls of the Bloody Tower. Another has it that not even dogs will go into the Salt Tower after dark, and a third asserts that a Yeoman Warder was once almost throttled by an unseen force. A different legend involves the well-cared-for Tower ravens. It is said that if they ever leave, the Tower and nation will fall.

VICTORIA & ALBERT MUSEUM

The exterior of the V&A has sculptures of established greats such as Turner, Constable, and Wren, a sharp contrast to the focal point of the entrance hall, a huge chandelier by Dale Chihuly (1999) with swirls of snakelike blue-and-green glass. The message is that both old and new are at home in this ultimate collection of decorative arts.

Decorative arts are anything and everything that adorns buildings and bodies. The fashion collection contains Dior outfits from the 1940s and Mary Quant's 1960s miniskirts; on display elsewhere are samurai armor and ancient weaponry that was as intricately decorated as it was deadly. In the India gallery, Tipoo's Tiger, a brightly colored carved wooden instrument, seems cute, although the tiger is mauling an Englishman. The reproduction of the 1st-century AD Trajan's Column in the Plaster Casts gallery has a frieze that measures 650 feet and features more than 2,500 sculpted figures, which look amazing close up. These are only some highlights to seek out.

KEEP IN MIND Allow more than two hours here. To stretch your visit, come on Wednesday, when the museum is open late. The downside is that generally just the ground floor is open at night and kids' backpacks aren't available.

EATS FOR KIDS The excellent **V&A Restaurant,** in the pretty brick-wall basement, has a budget-price "hungry monkey" kids' menu that lists such favorite staples as chicken, sausages, potatoes, and baked beans, followed by a daily dessert. On Sundays you can enjoy brunch or lunch while listening to music performed by students from the nearby Royal College of Music. **Patisserie Valerie** (215 Brompton Rd., tel. 020/7823–9971), in the direction of Harrods, serves pasta dishes of the day. It's famed for its mountainous chocolate cakes, but service can be a little curt.

V&A could easily stand for variety and activity, as the museum has free children's trail sheets and an activity cart with trays of fun things to do, such as making masks or pictures with paper, sequins, and shiny stick-ons. Each week the cart highlights a different section of the museum. To explore some of the 7 miles of galleries in depth, ask for a kids' activity backpack, filled with goody bags and folders to follow with an adult. In the Glass gallery, for instance, you feel objects while blindfolded and then hunt for the original, and put together a jigsaw. The only problem is choosing from the six backpacks available.

The cleverly presented British Galleries span four centuries (1500–1900), and each period has a kids' project corner. You can try on an Elizabethan ruff and an armor gauntlet, find out how to make an embroidered silk bag, or learn how to put together a Jacobean chair. The less handy can design a coat of arms on computer. In fact, there's so much to do here that kids (and grown-ups) will find it hard to squeeze in the rest of the museum.

HEY, KIDS! In the China gallery, look for a pair of cute silk embroidered slippers. You might think that they must have belonged to a doll, but the truth is that footwear like this was actually once worn by adult women. Their feet were bound at an early age so they would remain tiny enough to fit into shoes like this. (Needless to say, it wasn't very good for the feet.) Thankfully, foot binding is not practiced today.

WALLACE COLLECTION

4

ady Wallace left this wonderful collection of art to the nation in 1897, on the condition that admission would remain free, but that's just one of many reasons to visit. Another is the collection's setting: elegant Hertford House, an oasis of calm behind bustling Oxford Street. Walking around in the house and surveying the collection, which belonged to one family, the marquesses of Hertford, you feel as if you've received a prized invitation to tour the family heirlooms. The collection is known for its 18th-century French paintings and porcelain, and includes a brilliant concentration of famed artists of other nationalities—Canaletto, Rubens, Rembrandt, and Velázquez, to name a few. Prime among the must-see list is Frans Hals's *The Laughing Cavalier,* a jolly fellow indeed.

Trail booklets, available for a small price (80p–£1), invite parents and kids to walk around and talk about the paintings, furniture, and treasures and discover some fun facts. Adult notes let you help kids out and learn more yourself. Choose from the Monster trail; Paws

KEEP IN MIND Activity sessions during school vacations last 1½–2 hours and cost £5. Each is geared to a specified age range, and unless your kids are at the top of that range, they must be accompanied by an adult (who is not charged). To book in advance, call 020/7563–9551. Older kids might like the free, 20-minute Brief Encounter sessions, generally at 1, which celebrate one particular work. Free one-hour guided tours of the gallery depart Wednesday and Saturday at 11:30, Sunday at 3, and other days at 1. Times may change if there is a special lecture.

Hertford House, Manchester Sq., W1.
Tube: Bond St.

 Free

M-Sa 10-5, Su 12-5

020/7935-0687;
www.the-wallace-collection.org.uk

6 and up

and Claws, for younger kids; or Liberty, Equality and Fraternity, a family trail about the French Revolution, for older kids. On the subject of battle and strife, one of the best parts of the Wallace is secreted in the basement. Here you can see a superb collection of armor, containing the suits of many princes. If you want to see how different pieces might fit, head to the Conservation Room for a try.

To really visit the Wallace in a hands-on way, come when there's a children's activity session (about two hours; book in advance). Artists, sculptors, storytellers, and puppet makers help kids take a closer look at paintings with a particular theme, such as heroes and heroines or long-ago parties. Having been fired up with ideas from around the gallery, children produce their own piece of art. They may even get to try on some of that fabulous armor—all making for a memorable visit.

HEY, KIDS! Only people with loads of money could afford to have their portrait done by one of the top painters of the day, such as Velázquez or Rembrandt. And since you paid by the yard, only the extremely wealthy opted for life-size dimensions.

EATS FOR KIDS **Café Bagatelle** (tel. 020/7563–9505), in the bright courtyard, is a lovely place to eat, but it is pricey and not geared toward kids. Lunch costs around £20 per person. Luckily, there are many budget alternatives nearby among the sandwich bars and cafés behind Oxford Street and on Baker Street. You can also try **Wagamama** (101A Wigmore St., tel. 020/7409–0111), a stylish and inexpensive modern noodle bar (one of a popular chain). **Browns** (47 Maddox St., tel. 020/7491–4565) is well worth the walk for the all-day breakfast and memorable puds (puddings, meaning desserts), Brit-style.

WESTMINSTER ABBEY

A beautiful Early English Gothic showpiece with flying buttresses and sweeping arches, Westminster Abbey has hosted coronations since 1066 and is stuffed with royal tombs, monuments, and memorials to prominent people. From floor to fabulously decorated ceiling, there's plenty to admire.

The ancient Chapel of St. Edward (where the abbey's founder king is buried) is encircled by worn effigies of medieval monarchs, missing mosaic stones stolen for souvenirs over the centuries. Sadly, it's so fragile that you're not permitted inside. Beneath the steps to the Henry VII Chapel, the Coronation Chair bears the graffiti of naughty Westminster schoolboys. Inside the Henry VII Chapel, which is dominated by the tombs of King Henry and his queen (Elizabeth), Elizabeth I, her sister Mary I (beneath her), and Mary Queen of Scots (opposite aisle) are entombed as well. A marble urn holds the bones of the young princes presumed murdered in the Tower of London (*see #6*), and choir stalls contain curious carved creatures. Poets' Corner is crammed full of memorials and visitors.

HEY, KIDS!
Take a closer look and see if you can find little round splotches in the granite pillars. They're actually fossilized mollusks—just one of the neat details to discover here.

EATS FOR KIDS Victoria Street has chain eateries from pizza places to coffee shops and burger joints. The **Wesley Café** (tel. 020/7222–8010) is a popular budget haunt opposite the abbey, in Central Hall, Storey's Gate. In the crypt of this former Methodist church you can grab a hot or cold meal for around £5. The pine-and-glass Army and Navy department store **restaurant** (101 Victoria St., tel. 020/7834–1234) is light and airy. Children's meals consist of fries with sausages, chicken nuggets, or fish sticks. For parents, a daily changing menu includes vegetarian dishes from £5. Also see Royal Mews at Buckingham Palace.

Broad Sanctuary, SW1.
Tube: Westminster

 Abbey and museum
£6 ages 16 and up, £2.50
children 11–15

Abbey M–F 9:30–3:45 (W until 6), Sa 9–1:45,
closed for some services; museum daily 10–4;
College Garden Tu–Th 10–4

020/7222–5152;
www.westminster-abbey.org

 6 and up

Noteworthy denizens are Handel, Dickens, Byron, Oscar Wilde, and Shakespeare. Scientists Newton, Darwin, and Livingstone are in the nave, near Ben Jonson (buried standing up, per his wishes, but without a coffin as he couldn't afford one). The Tomb of the Unknown Warrior is near eight volumes listing citizens who died during the Blitz during World War II.

The Abbey Museum almost brings tomb residents to life through startlingly realistic effigies: Henry VII's was taken from his death mask; Charles II's, equally realistic, is richly adorned; and Elizabeth I's is displayed in underwear. Search for the ring she gave to her favorite, the earl of Essex, along with its romantic story. The medieval Chapter House (where a chapter from the Scriptures was read daily) is octagonal, with wooden seats encircling the original tiled floor. Joining these rooms to the abbey, the little cloister garden is a quiet haven where you can reflect on the rich history of this ancient place. Even larger, the College Garden was tended by monks for over 900 years. Open midweek, it's a secret place for you to explore and breathe in the aromas of medicinal herbs.

KEEP IN MIND Photography is not allowed within the abbey, but pictures can be found in the stunning color guidebooks and postcards on sale at the Abbey Bookshop, outside the west entrance, and in the Abbey Museum. These show many of the sacred and ancient places not often open to visitors, such as St. Edward's Chapel. If you particularly want to take a closer look at these areas, sign up for a Verger tour for an extra charge. Phone for information, or check on the information board outside the entrance.

WIMBLEDON LAWN TENNIS MUSEUM

For two weeks in June each year, Britons and other fans are gripped with tennis fever, as the titans slug it out on grass in one of the world's most coveted tennis championships. When it all began, in the early 1900s, there were no professionals and no big prize monies. Back then tennis was a genteel, fashionable game for the upper classes, a craze on the lawns of polite society in Victorian England. The club held its own informal amateur championships among about 10 participants. Today those who love the game can make a pilgrimage to this museum and tennis mecca.

You can browse through all sorts of memorabilia, including paintings and posters. A children's corner contains objects to engage them: for instance, how fast could Andy Roddick serve with a funny-looking wooden racket with gappy strings rather than titanium technology? You can gaze upon the authentic championship trophies and marvel that, in the old amateur days, after all that sweaty effort, the winners only got a medal. In the dress collection, check out the old-time outfits from more than 100 years ago, which look

EATS FOR KIDS The **Café Centre Court** is open year-round and serves snacks, lunch, and traditional teas in a nostalgic setting of wood paneling, murals, and conservatory-style furniture. Options on the High Street in Wimbledon village are many. They include **Starbucks** (82 High St., tel. 020/8947–5577), **Pizza Express** (84 High St., tel. 020/8946–6027), and **Marzano** (8 High St., tel. 020/8944–6893), a buzzy pasta restaurant, among many coffee shops and sandwich bars.

as if they were meant for a posh picnic. The skimpiest Venus Williams creation is on show, if you want to speculate on how she would play in ankle-length linen instead of skimpy Lycra. A model shows how Wimbledon looked in the early 20th century, videos let you relive great games of the past (including the past year's finals), and an interactive quiz tests your knowledge of the tournament and its competitors. You can even try to buy tickets for next year's tournament, but good luck! You must apply in writing, months in advance, just to enter the drawing for tickets.

You can ask questions of guides in old-style tennis gear who are on hand to highlight the displays. An even better idea is to reserve a spot in one of the small-group tours. In addition to seeing the museum, you get a real peek behind the scenes, get close to the show courts' sacred turf, and take a look around the broadcast studios. It may be the closest you'll be to Centre Court unless your tennis game improves dramatically.

HEY, KIDS! Strawberries and cream are synonymous with Wimbledon, like hot dogs and baseball. Come rain or shine, the championships pretty much herald the start of the English strawberry-eating season. Each year at the tournament, a mountainous 23 tons of strawberries are consumed—at a price, of course!

KEEP IN MIND During the championships, the museum is accessible to tournament visitors only and is open until the close of play each day. (It's a good place to linger during the inevitable rain delays.) Some facilities may be restricted during this time. To apply for the public ticket ballot for next year's tournament, check the Web site and send in your written request for an application form no later than December 31. Your completed form enters you in the draw for tickets.

WINDSOR CASTLE

In 1080, William the Conqueror chose a good place for his fortress, close to the Thames and London. Though the stone castle has grown much over the centuries, it remains the only castle constantly used by the royal family since William's day. Today it still dominates the landscape, towering above the pretty town of old Windsor and neighboring Eton, across the Thames, and it can clearly be seen from the freeway heading west from London. Whether viewed from inside or out, Windsor Castle is spectacular.

Children do find parts of the castle interior fascinating. The fabulously ornate State Apartments contain old master paintings, chintz, china, and chandeliers galore, but the Grand Staircase and Vestibule's old weaponry—shiny swords, muskets, and rifles in cases, and crisscrossed weapons hung on very high walls—will probably entice kids far more. You can see Henry VIII's armor of massive girth and the very bullet that killed Lord Nelson at the Battle of Trafalgar. One of the oldest rooms, St. George's Hall, was beautifully restored after a fire in 1992. It's lined with suits of knightly armor bearing lances pointing

HEY, KIDS!

Like all the royals, Britain's queens have retreated to Windsor Castle. Queen Victoria and her nine children got away from smoky London on the new steam railway and received diplomats and dignitaries here. You'll know the current Queen is in if the Royal Standard is flying.

KEEP IN MIND It's worth phoning to check on opening times and discover whether the State Apartments are closed for a royal banquet. Arrive early to avoid lines, and give yourself time to absorb the charms of old Windsor and Eton. Even if you don't visit the castle, you can spend a lovely day at the Eton Brocas, the pretty meadows sloping down to the river, where you can watch boats, royal swans, and ducks go by, or in the extensive grounds of Windsor Great Park, where you might catch a polo match or spy a herd of shy deer in the old royal hunting grounds.

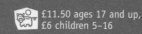

Windsor Park, Berkshire.
Rail: Windsor

£11.50 ages 17 and up,
£6 children 5–16

020/7766-7304;
www.royal.gov.uk

Mar–Oct, daily 9:45–5:15 (last entry 4);
Nov–Feb, daily 9:45–4:15 (last entry 3)

All ages

up to the ceiling, which is emblazoned with the coats of arms of all the Knights of the Garter. At one end, the royal champion knight is poised, gauntlet raised, ready to throw down a challenge; this wasn't a usual occurrence but rather a coronation ritual.

The most charming item is a dollhouse made for Queen Mary (Queen Elizabeth's grandmother), at the entrance to the State Apartments. Absolutely everything in the mansion was a faithful copy of 1924 furnishings, all of which work, from the electric lights and elevators to the gramophone. The cellar contains vintage wine, and books and paintings were produced by the authors and artists themselves. What little girl could resist playing with these minitreasures? It is positively enchanting, as are the larger dolls' trousseaux belonging to the young princesses Elizabeth and Margaret; designed by Dior and other great couturiers of the 1930s, they are displayed in the adjoining room.

EATS FOR KIDS There is nothing to eat within the castle, but old Windsor has plenty of choices. In the Fenwick department store, the **Terrace Café** (King Edward Ct., tel. 01753/855537), off Peascod Street and opposite Castle Hill, has a menu that changes daily. You can get half-portions for kids of some dishes, including the usual favorite of sausage and fries. The friendly, old-world **Drury House** (4 Church St., tel. 01753/863734) has wood paneling, fireplaces, English roasts, and traditional teas.

CLASSIC GAMES

"I SEE SOMETHING YOU DON'T SEE AND IT IS BLUE." Stuck for a way to get your youngsters to settle down in a museum? Sit them down on a bench in the middle of a room and play this vintage favorite. The leader gives just one clue—the color—and everybody guesses away.

"I'M GOING TO THE GROCERY..." The first player begins, "I'm going to the grocery and I'm going to buy... " and finishes the sentence with the name of an object, found in grocery stores, that begins with the letter "A." The second player repeats what the first player has said, and adds the name of another item that starts with "B." The third player repeats everything that has been said so far and adds something that begins with "C" and so on through the alphabet. Anyone who skips or misremembers an item is out (or decide up front that you'll give hints to all who need 'em). You can modify the theme depending on where you're going that day, as "I'm going to X and I'm going to see..."

FAMILY ARK Noah had his ark—here's your chance to build your own. It's easy: Just start naming animals and work your way through the alphabet, from antelope to zebra.

PLAY WHILE YOU WAIT

NOT THE GOOFY GAME Have one child name a category. (Some ideas: first names, last names, animals, countries, friends, feelings, foods, hot or cold things, clothing.) Then take turns naming things that fall into that category. You're out if you name something that doesn't belong in the category—or if you can't think of another item to name. When only one person remains, start again. Choose categories depending on where you're going or where you've been—historic topics if you've seen a historic sight, animal topics before or after the zoo, upside-down things if you've been to the circus, and so on. Make the game harder by choosing category items in A-B-C order.

DRUTHERS How do your kids really feel about things? Just ask. "Would you rather eat worms or hamburgers? Hamburgers or candy?" Choose serious and silly topics—and have fun!

BUILD A STORY "Once upon a time there lived..." Finish the sentence and ask the rest of your family, one at a time, to add another sentence or two. Bring a tape recorder along to record the narrative—and you can enjoy your creation again and again.

GOOD TIMES GALORE

WIGGLE & GIGGLE Give your kids a chance to stick out their tongues at you. Start by making a face, then have the next person imitate you and add a gesture of his own—snapping fingers, winking, clapping, sneezing, or the like. The next person mimics the first two and adds a third gesture, and so on.

JUNIOR OPERA During a designated period of time, have your kids sing everything they want to say.

THE QUIET GAME Need a good giggle—or a moment of calm to figure out your route? The driver sets a time limit and everybody must be silent. The last person to make a sound wins.

THE A-LIST

BEST IN TOWN
British Airways London Eye
Museum in Docklands
Natural History Museum
Tate Modern
Tower of London

BEST OUTDOORS
Legoland
Hawk Conservancy

BEST CULTURAL ACTIVITY
Hampton Court Palace

BEST MUSEUM
Science Museum

WACKIEST
London Dungeon

NEW & NOTEWORTHY
London Wetland Centre

SOMETHING FOR EVERYONE

A LITTLE KNOWLEDGE
Bank of England Museum, 66
Brass Rubbing Centre, 63
British Library, 61
Kew Bridge Steam Museum, 42
Museum in Docklands, 30
Royal National Theatre, 19
Shakespeare's Globe, 15
Thames Barrier Visitor Centre, 10
Theatre Museum, 9
Westminster Abbey, 3

ART ATTACK
Art 4 Fun, 67
Courtauld Gallery, 55
Kenwood House, 43
National Gallery, 27
National Portrait Gallery, 25
Somerset House, 14
Tate Britain, 12
Tate Modern, 11
Victoria & Albert Museum, 5
Wallace Collection, 4

COOL 'HOODS
Covent Garden, 54
Regent's Canal, 23

CULTURE CLUB
The British Museum, 60
Museum of London, 29
Shakespeare's Globe, 15
Tate Britain, 12
Theatre Museum, 9
Victoria & Albert Museum, 5

FARMS & ANIMALS
Aquatic Experience, 68
Camley Street Natural Park, 58
Chessington World of Adventures, 56
Hawk Conservancy, 47
London Aquarium, 40
London Wetland Centre, 36
London Zoo, 35

FREEBIES
Bank of England Museum, 66
Brass Rubbing Centre, 63

British Library, **61**
The British Museum, **60**
Changing of the Guard, **57**
Covent Garden, **54**
Greenwich Park, **50**
Hampstead Heath, **49**
Imperial War Museum, **45**
Kensington Gardens, **44**
Kenwood House, **43**
Millennium Bridge, **33**
Museum of London, **29**
National Army Museum, **28**
National Gallery, **27**
National Maritime Museum, **26**
National Portrait Gallery, **25**
Natural History Museum, **24**
Regent's Park, **22**
Science Museum, **16**
Somerset House, **14**
Tate Britain, **12**
Tate Modern, **11**
Victoria & Albert Museum, **5**
Wallace Collection, **4**

GAMES AND AMUSEMENTS

Chessington World of Adventures, **56**
Legoland, **41**
Thorpe Park, *8*

HISTORICAL

Bank of England Museum, **66**
Bekonscot Model Village, **65**
Brass Rubbing Centre, **63**
British Library, **61**
Cabinet War Rooms, **59**
Cutty Sark, **53**
Firepower!, **52**
Golden Hinde, **51**
Hampton Court Palace, **48**
HMS *Belfast*, **46**
Imperial War Museum, **45**
London Dungeon, **38**
London's Transport Museum, **37**
Madame Tussaud's & London Planetarium, **34**
Monument, **32**
Mountfitchet Castle, **31**

Museum in Docklands, **30**
Museum of London, **29**
National Army Museum, **28**
National Maritime Museum, **26**
Royal Mews at Buckingham Palace, **20**
St. Paul's Cathedral, **17**
Shakespeare's Globe, **15**
Tower Bridge Experience, **7**
Tower of London, **6**
Westminster Abbey, **3**
Windsor Castle, **1**

IT'S A WACKY WORLD
London Dungeon, **38**
Madame Tussaud's & London
Planetarium, **34**

LOST IN SPACE
Madame Tussaud's & London
Planetarium, **34**
Royal Observatory, **18**

PARKS AND GARDENS
Camley Street Natural Park, **58**
Greenwich Park, **50**

Hampstead Heath, **49**
Hampton Court Palace, **48**
Kensington Gardens, **44**
Kenwood House, **43**
Regent's Park, **23**
Royal Botanic Gardens, **21**
Syon Park, **13**

PERFORMANCES
BFI London IMAX Cinema, **64**
Covent Garden, **54**
Hampton Court Palace, **48**
National Army Museum, **28**
Regent's Park, **22**
Royal National Theatre, **19**
Shakespeare's Globe, **15**
Somerset House, **14**
Theatre Museum, **9**

PLANES, TRAINS, AND AUTOMOBILES
Kew Bridge Steam Museum, **42**
London's Transport Museum, **37**
Science Museum, **16**

RAINY DAYS

Art 4 Fun, **67**
Bank of England Museum, **66**
BFI London IMAX Cinema, **64**
British Library, **61**
The British Museum, **60**
Cabinet War Rooms, **59**
Courtauld Gallery, **55**
Firepower, **52**
Imperial War Museum, **45**
Kew Bridge Steam Museum, **42**
London Aquarium, **40**
London's Transport Museum, **37**
Madame Tussaud's & London Planetarium, **34**
Museum in Docklands, **30**
Museum of London, **29**
National Gallery, **27**
National Maritime Museum, **26**
National Portrait Gallery, **25**
Natural History Museum, **24**
Science Museum, **16**
Tate Britain, **12**
Tate Modern, **11**
Theatre Museum, **9**
Westminster Abbey, **3**

SCIENCE SCENES

BFI London IMAX Cinema, **64**
Kew Bridge Steam Museum, **42**
London Aquarium, **40**
London Butterfly House, **39**
Madame Tussaud's & London Planetarium, **34**
Natural History Museum, **24**
Royal Observatory, **18**
Science Museum, **16**

SPORTS STOPS

Wimbledon Lawn Tennis Museum, **2**

TINIEST TOTS

Aquatic Experience, **68**
Bekonscot Model Village, **65**
British Airways London Eye, **62**
Changing of the Guard, **57**
Chessington World of Adventures, **56**
Covent Garden, **54**
Greenwich Park, **50**
Hampstead Heath, **49**
Kensington Gardens, **44**
Kenwood House, **43**

Legoland, 41
London Aquarium, 40
London Butterfly House, 39
London Zoo, 35
Millennium Bridge, 33
Regent's Canal, 23
Regent's Park, 22
Royal Botanic Gardens, 21
Science Museum, 16
Syon Park, 13
Thorpe Park, 8
Windsor Castle, 1

TIRE THEM OUT
Chessington World of Adventures, 56
Thorpe Park, 8

WATER, WATER EVERYWHERE
Aquatic Experience, 68
Cutty Sark, 53

Golden Hinde, 51
HMS *Belfast*, 46
London Aquarium, 40
Millennium Bridge, 33
Museum in Docklands, 30
National Maritime Museum, 26
Regent's Canal, 23
Thames Barrier Visitor Centre, 10
Thorpe Park, 8

WAY UP HIGH
British Airways London Eye, 62
Chessington World of Adventures, 56
Hampstead Heath, 49
Millennium Bridge, 33
Monument, 32
St. Paul's Cathedral, 17
Tower Bridge Experience, 7

ALL AROUND TOWN

BLOOMSBURY/EUSTON
British Library, **61**
The British Museum, **60**
Camley Street Natural Park, **58**

THE CITY
Bank of England Museum, **66**
Millennium Bridge, **33**
Monument, **32**
Museum of London, **29**
St. Paul's Cathedral, **17**
Tower Bridge Experience, **7**
Tower of London, **6**

COVENT GARDEN
Brass Rubbing Centre, **63**
Courtauld Gallery, **55**
Covent Garden, **54**
London's Transport Museum, **37**
Somerset House, **14**
Theatre Museum, **9**

GREENWICH/DOCKLANDS
Cutty Sark, **53**
Museum in Docklands, **30**

Greenwich Park, **50**
National Maritime Museum, **26**
Royal Observatory, **18**

KENSINGTON/ NOTTING HILL
Art 4 Fun, **67**
Kensington Gardens, **44**

REGENT'S PARK/ HAMPSTEAD
Hampstead Heath, **49**
Kenwood House, **43**
London Zoo, **35**
Madame Tussaud's & London Planetarium, **34**
Regent's Canal, **23**
Regent's Park, **22**

SOUTH BANK
BFI London IMAX Cinema, **64**
British Airways London Eye, **62**
Golden Hinde, **51**
HMS *Belfast*, **46**

Imperial War Museum, **45**
London Aquarium, **40**
London Dungeon, **38**
Millennium Bridge, **33**
Royal National Theatre, **19**
Shakespeare's Globe, **15**
Tate Modern, **11**

SOUTH KENSINGTON/ CHELSEA

National Army Museum, **28**
Natural History Museum, **24**
Science Museum, **16**
Victoria & Albert Museum, **5**

WESTMINSTER/ MAYFAIR

Cabinet War Rooms, **59**
Changing of the Guard, **57**
National Gallery, **27**
National Portrait Gallery, **25**
Royal Mews at Buckingham Palace, **20**
Tate Britain, **12**
Wallace Collection, **4**
Westminster Abbey, **3**

WOOLWICH

Firepower, **52**
Thames Barrier Visitor Centre, **10**

SOUTHWEST LONDON

London Wetland Centre, **36**
Wimbledon Lawn Tennis Museum, **2**

OUTSIDE LONDON

Aquatic Experience, **68**
Bekonscot Model Village, **65**
Chessington World of Adventures, **56**
Hampton Court Palace, **48**
Hawk Conservancy, **47**
Kew Bridge Steam Museum, **42**
Legoland, **41**
London Butterfly House, **39**
Mountfitchet Castle, **31**
Royal Botanic Gardens, **21**
Syon Park, **13**
Thorpe Park, **8**
Windsor Castle, **1**

MANY THANKS!

More than once I thought my two children would rebel as I faced them with yet another jam-packed weekend of visiting brilliant places in pursuit of the quintessential review. They didn't—rebel, that is—and had a ball, and so did their parents, who got to see many familiar sights in interesting new ways. So thank you, kids, for your enthusiasm and endurance during my persnickety investigations. My son was convinced I would turn into a *National Geographic* reporter as I picked up the trail of a new find. In the end, the limit of 68 places doesn't quite do London justice.

We also enjoyed especially attentive treatment from many attractions' education and information people, whose expert advice was a boon—in particular, the staff of the Museum in Docklands, Bekonscot Model Village, London Wetland Centre, Westminster Abbey, and English Heritage at the abbey's Chapter House. You provided a real personal touch. The press and publicity departments who insured that information packs were in the right place at the right time are too many to mention, as are the friends, relatives, and their children who reported faithfully on their missions and came back for more. What a team! I am sure that the fruits of your labors will make other visitors' experiences all the more enjoyable.

—Jacqueline Brown